Primary
Maths
in Action

Pupil Book

Irene Hogg

Robin Howat

David McNulty

Eddie Mullan

Ken Nisbet

Sandra White

Published in 2003 by:
Nelson Thornes Ltd
Delta Place
27 Bath Road
CHELTENHAM
GL53 7TH
United Kingdom

03 04 05 / 10 9 8 7 6 5 4 3 2 1

A catalogue record for this book is available from the British Library

ISBN 0–7487–7706–7

Design, Illustration and Typesetting by J&L Composition, Filey, North Yorkshire

Printed in Great Britain by Scotprint

Contents

Block 4

Unit 1 — Whole Numbers

For thousands of years people have used numbers to record things. The numbers we use today are thought to have been invented in India and brought to Europe in the 8th century BC by Arab traders and travellers.

1 Looking Back

1. Write the heights of these four Scottish mountains in words:

Mountain	Height (m)
Ben Nevis	1344 metres
Ben Macdhui	1309 metres
Ben Lawers	1214 metres
Carn Mairg	1042 metres

2. Write the height of these mountains in figures:

Mountain	Height (m)
Mount Everest (Asia)	eight thousand, eight hundred and fifty metres
Mount Kilimanjaro (Africa)	five thousand, eight hundred and ninety metres
Mont Blanc (Europe)	four thousand, eight hundred and seven metres
Mount Aconcagua (S. America)	six thousand, nine hundred and sixty metres

3. These are the mileometer readings on four cars:

a 7 9 8 9   b 6 2 9 9   c 3 9 9 9   d 9 0 6 9

Write down the readings after the cars have travelled one more mile.

4. What number do you subtract from 3647 to give you:

a 3640   b 3607   c 3547   d 3047?

5. What number do you add to 8512 to give you:

a 8520   b 8592   c 8602   d 9012?

6. Using each of the digits once:

6 1 7 4

a What is the largest number you can form?

b What is the smallest number you can form?

c Write these largest and smallest numbers in words.

7. Sam has five raffle tickets:

Put the tickets in order, smallest first.

7710 7065 PM1 JL2

7609 PM1 JL2 **6979** PM1 JL2 *6980* PM1 JL2

Do questions 8–10 without written working.

8. a 25 + 9   b 97 + 6   c 85 – 7   d 68 – 9

   e 132 + 8   f 457 + 5   g 632 – 6   h 274 – 8

   i 260 + 30   j 110 – 50   k 540 – 90   l 430 – 70

9. Chloe's holiday costs £105. She has £93. How much *more* money does Chloe need?

10. A milk lorry can carry 240 crates of milk. There are 180 crates of milk on the lorry. How many more crates can the lorry carry?

11. Calculate:

   a   623   b   538   c   786   d   473   e   808   f   243
      + 56   + 17   – 42   – 58   + 97   – 38

12. Calculate:

   a 874 + 63   b 326 – 54   c 679 + 82   d 520 – 36

13. There are 324 pupils at Sunnyside Primary School. 46 of the pupils are left-handed. 65 have blue eyes. 97 have fair hair. How many pupils:

   a are right-handed?

   b do not have blue eyes?

   c do not have fair hair?

14. Molly and her mum have a Jetset holiday to Cyprus.

   a What is the total cost?

   b How much cheaper is Molly's holiday than her mum's?

JETSET
Holidays to Cyprus
Adult   Child
£245   £95

15.

£275

£89

£149

3 brand new
computer games

a What is the total cost of *Moon Wars* and *Son of Kong*?

b What is the difference in price between the dearest and the cheapest game?

2 Going Big with Numbers

49 152 forty-nine thousand, one hundred and fifty-two

627 538 six hundred and twenty-seven thousand, five hundred and thirty-eight

	Thousands				
Hundreds	Tens	Units	Hundreds	Tens	Units
	4	9	1	5	2
6	2	7	5	3	8

When we have more than four digits, we leave a gap at the point where we say 'thousand'.

 A

1. 98 342   **2.** 12 065   **3.** 386 701   **4.** 570 683

In 98 342   There are 98 thousands. How many:

     a thousands   **b** hundreds   **c** tens   **d** units

     are there in each number?

5. Write the numbers from questions 1–4 in words.

6. The table shows the number of babies born in Scotland in 1901 and in 2001.

Year	Girls	Boys	Total
1901	64 439	67 753	132 192
2001	30 128	28 076	58 204

Write in words:

a the number of girls born: i in 1901   ii in 2001

b the number of boys born: i in 1901   ii in 2001

c the total number of babies born in Scotland: i in 1901   ii in 2001

7. The number of motorbikes in Scotland in 1995 was *twenty-three thousand, eight hundred and seventy-five*. In 2005 the number was *thirty thousand and sixty-five*. Write both numbers in figures.

8. Write the populations of these five towns in figures.

9.

Town	Population
Inverness	forty-one thousand, two hundred and thirty-four
East Kilbride	seventy thousand, four hundred and twenty-two
Irvine	thirty-two thousand, nine hundred and eighty-eight
Greenock	fifty-five thousand and thirteen
Polmont	eighteen thousand, four hundred and one

The table gives the populations of the four largest cities in Scotland.

Write down the populations in words.

City	Glasgow	Edinburgh	Aberdeen	Dundee
Population	660 954	401 910	189 707	158 981

10. a The number of visitors to Edinburgh Zoo last year was five hundred and sixty-two thousand, seven hundred and twelve.

b The number of visitors to Stirling Castle was four hundred and thirty thousand, six hundred and twenty-five.

c The number of visitors to Glenturret was two hundred and seventeen thousand, eight hundred and five.

Write each of these three numbers as figures.

Welcome to

EDINBURGH
ZOO
Scotland's most exciting
wildlife attraction

| Where are we? | Who are we? |

11. The table shows the number of overseas visitors to Scotland from some countries in the year 2000.

Write each of the numbers of visitors in words.

Country	Number of visitors
USA	406 375
Germany	237 050
France	152 725
Canada	130 500

12. The total attendance for the season at the 'home' matches of some Scottish Premier League football teams are given below.

Team Attendance

Aberdeen	two hundred and forty thousand, one hundred and four
Celtic	eight hundred and seventy-three thousand, five hundred and eighty-two
Hearts	two hundred and seventy-six thousand and seventy-four
Hibs	two hundred and six thousand, five hundred and twenty-four
Rangers	nine hundred and five thousand, one hundred and two

Write these attendances in figures.

3 Counting on Numbers

1. 30 657 people bought tickets to see the Pell-Mells perform live.

Change the number of people to:

a 1 more	**d** 10 more	**g** 10 less
b 2 more	**e** 100 more	**h** 100 less
c 3 more	**f** 1000 more	**i** 1000 less

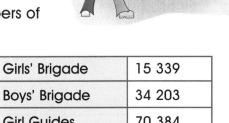

2. The table shows the number of Scottish members of each youth organisation.

a Write each of the numbers in words.

b Change the number in the Girls' Brigade to:
  i 1 more **ii** 10 more **iii** 100 less

Girls' Brigade	15 339
Boys' Brigade	34 203
Girl Guides	70 384
Scouts	39 060

c To the number in the Boys' Brigade:
   i add 10   **ii** add 10 000   **iii** take away 100

d To the number in the Girl Guides:
   i add 10   **ii** add 20   **iii** add 1000   **iv** take away 1000

e To the number in the Scouts:
   i subtract 1   **ii** subtract 100   **iii** add 1000

f 900 of the Scouts are girls. Find the number of boy Scouts.

3. Five children held up their favourite single-digit number.

  a Find the largest five-digit number that can be formed using each digit once.

  b Find the smallest number that can be formed using each digit once.

  c Find the largest number with 2 in the thousands column.

4. They were then asked about their *second* favourite digit.

  a Find the largest five-digit number from this collection, using each digit once.

  b Find the smallest number from this collection, using each digit once.

  c Find the smallest number with 1 in the hundreds column.

  d What is the largest even number that can be formed?

  e What is the smallest odd number?

Challenge   ④ ⑨ ④ ⑨ ④

1. Write down:
   a the largest number that can be formed using each digit once.
   b the smallest number that can be formed using each digit once.

2. List all the possible five-digit numbers that can be formed using each digit once.

3. Put them in order, starting with the largest.

5. List the populations of the towns in order of size, starting with the largest.

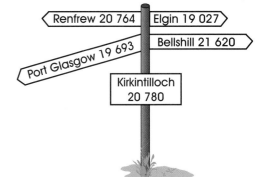

Renfrew 20 764 Elgin 19 027
Port Glasgow 19 693 Bellshill 21 620
Kirkintilloch 20 780

6. Find its population if:

a Renfrew had one thousand less
b Kirkintilloch had one less
c Port Glasgow had ten more
d Elgin had one hundred less.

4 ▸ Making Numbers Count

1. Calculate:

a	432	b	715	c	2607	d	5814
	+ 167		+ 268		+ 359		+ 2736

e	5708	f	6357	g	9375	h	7068
	+ 1368		+ 2384		+ 9815		+ 5326

i 2467 + 3184   j 537 + 6291   k 8039 + 784

l 4321 + 1647 + 3455   m 4529 + 2328 + 635   n 1163 + 5387 + 3072

2. The dairy delivered 354 bottles of milk yesterday and 479 bottles today. How many bottles of milk were delivered altogether?

3. Last month the number of male swimmers at the swimming pool was 6087. The number of female swimmers was 5645. Find the number of male swimmers plus the number of female swimmers.

Item	Profit
Bread	£3281
Cakes	£1764
Buns	£2036

4. The table shows the profits made by the baker.

Calculate the total profit.

5. Three lengths of wire are 4671 cm, 2085 cm and 745 cm. Find the sum of the three lengths of wire.

6. Calculate:

a	736 − 215	b	653 − 148	c	670 − 438	d	700 − 267	e	5374 − 2636
f	9615 − 3279	g	8111 − 3504	h	7340 − 6816	i	4056 − 1729	j	2975 − 638

7. On Friday, Fresco Supermarket had 528 customers. On Saturday, there were 715 customers. How many more customers were there on Saturday?

8. Bev's best score at the game of *Dok* is 7625. Billy's best score is 5908. What is the difference in their scores?

9. Five years ago the population of Cherrytown was 3724. This year it is 4607. Find the increase in the population.

10. The length of the Old Course at St Andrew's is 6566 yards. The length of the Royal Troon golf course is 6641 yards. How much shorter is the course at St Andrew's?

11. Polly bought a painting for £3625 and sold it for £8250. Calculate Polly's profit.

12. Mike has 3450 stamps. Meg has 986 stamps fewer than Mike. How many stamps does Meg have?

13. Calculate:

   a 4371 + 4083 − 6718   b 6534 − 2806 + 7593   c 8461 − 2409 − 3175

14. 8621 runners started a marathon. Only 5846 of them finished. How many runners dropped out?

B

1. Last week the baker baked 832 loaves and 8225 rolls.

   a What is the sum of the loaves and rolls baked?

   b What is the difference between the number of rolls and loaves baked?

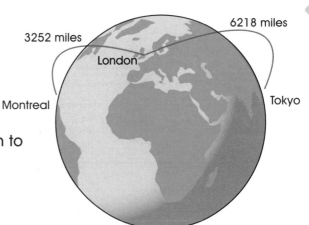

2. a How much further is it from London to Tokyo than from London to Montreal?

   b Julie flew from Montreal to London and then from London to Tokyo. How far did Julie fly altogether?

3. The school library has 4714 fiction books, 2367 non-fiction books and 1095 reference books.

   a How many more fiction books are there than non-fiction books?

   b What is the total number of fiction and non-fiction books?

   c How many books are there altogether in the library?

4. The table shows the number of people who bought tickets to see Mother Goose at the Palace Theatre.

   a What was the total number of adult tickets bought?

   b How many more tickets in the Stalls were bought for children than for adults?

   c How many tickets were bought altogether for the Circle?

   d How many tickets were bought in total for the Stalls?

   e How many fewer tickets for the Circle were bought than for the Stalls?

   f How many tickets were sold altogether?

	Stalls	Circle
Adults	2368	1965
Children	4073	2396

Unit 2 Angles

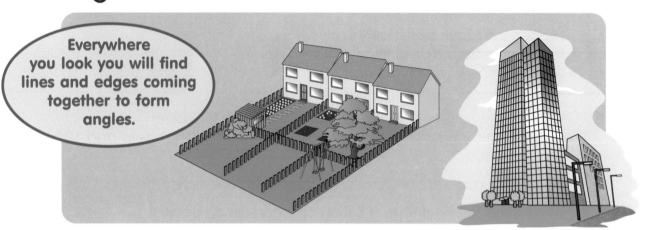

Everywhere you look you will find lines and edges coming together to form angles.

1 Looking Back

An angle less than 90° is called acute

An angle more than 90° but less than 180° is called obtuse

1. **a** Fold a piece of paper to form a crease. Fold along this crease to form a right angle.

   b Use your right angle to identify the right angles in the following pictures:

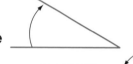

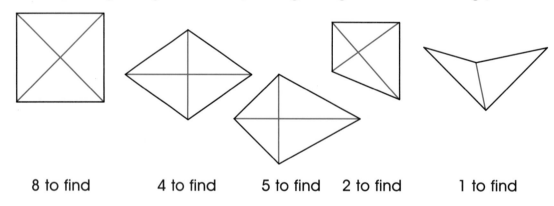

| 8 to find | 4 to find | 5 to find | 2 to find | 1 to find |

2. What type of angle is each of the following?

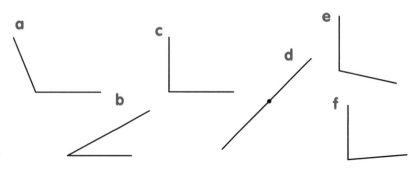

3. At the fair, the balloon is tethered by a rope. As the wind gets up the angle between the rope and the tower changes. What type of angle is being made at each stage?

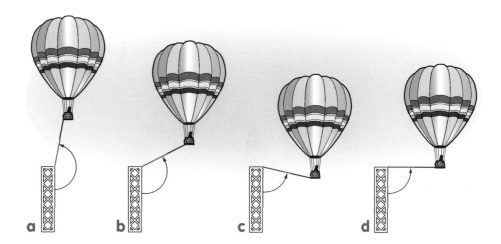

a   b   c   d

4. What size of angle is shown on each clock?

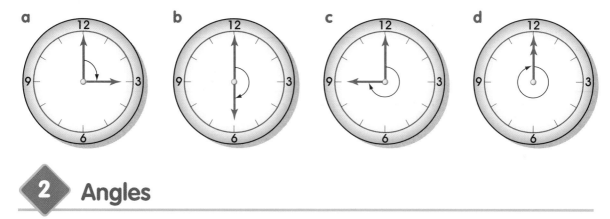

a   b   c   d

2   Angles

Angles can be used to describe shape.

They can also be used to describe a turning or rotation.

Example 1
The slope of the ski run is describing a shape.

Example 2
The marked angle will describe the turn made by the plane.

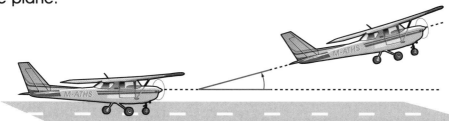

A

1. Look at each situation and decide whether the marked angle is describing a rotation or a shape.

A quarter turn is 90°
Half a turn is 180°
A complete turn is 360°

a

b

c

d

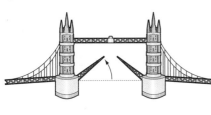

e

f

2. To fully open, the door turns through 90°.

   How many degrees does it turn through:

   a when it is half open

   b when it is open one third of the way?

   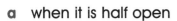
   closed

   open

   view from above

   closed

   half open

   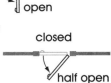

3. In one hour the minute hand of the clock turns through 360°. It is pointing at 12.

   a To reach the 3, it has to go through a quarter of a turn. What size of angle is this?

   b To reach the 1, the hand goes through one twelfth of a turn. What size of angle is this?

   c What size is the turn when the hand goes from 12 to:
   i 2   **ii** 4   **iii** 8   **iv** 9?

4. To get round a corner safely, the biker has to lean over. At what angle is the biker leaning in each case?

a

half a right angle

b

a tenth of a right angle

c

a fifth of a right angle

3 Naming Things

A, B and C are three points.

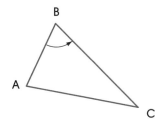

AB, BC and CA are three lines which form the triangle ABC.

The angle marked by an arc is called ∠ ABC or ∠ CBA.

The vertex of the angle is B – it is the middle letter in the name.

The arms of the angle are AB and BC.

1. In each diagram, name:

   i   the point being pointed to

   ii   the angle

   iii the arms of the angle

   iv   the vertex of the angle.

a

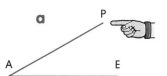

b

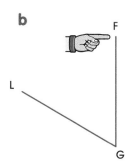

c

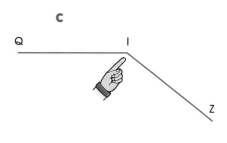

d

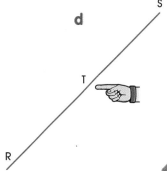

2. **a** Name each of the angles below.

 b Use tracing paper to help you decide which angle is the biggest.

 c Which is smaller, ∠ ABC or ∠ DHT?

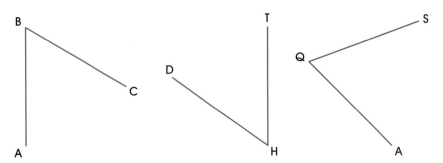

3. The sea plane is coming in to land. It will make a safe landing if the angle marked is less than 15°.

 a What is the name of this type of angle?

 b Is the angle shown a safe angle?

 c By how many degrees must it change to be exactly 15°?

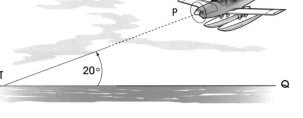

4. The sail is a triangle   LMN. The angle MLN = 60°.

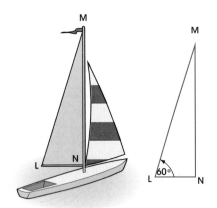

 a Name the angle which has its vertex at M.

 b Name two different angles which have an arm called MN.

 c One of the angles is a right angle and one is 30°.
   i Name the right angle.
   ii Name the 30° angle.

B

1. Newtown has a public park. On the right is a map of the park.

    The rectangle ABCD represents the park fence.

    PR is a path through the park.

    It passes by a fountain at the point F.

    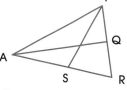

    a   Copy the map into your jotter.

    b   ∠ BAF = 35°. Mark this on your drawing.

    c   ∠ ADF = 55°. Mark this on your drawing.

    d   ∠ PAB = 90°. Name three other right angles.

    e   Frank walks his dog. He enters the park at A. The path he takes forms a straight angle.
    i   Name the straight angle.
    ii   What is at the vertex of the straight angle?

2. In the diagram we can name three angles with a vertex at A.

    These are ∠ PAQ, ∠ QAR and ∠ PAR.

    a   There are three angles with a vertex at P. Name them.

    b   There are three angles with a vertex at Q. Name them.

    c   How many angles have AR as an arm?

Challenge

Disaster! The high winds have ruined Mary's brolly.

There is nothing left but the ribs!

How many angles, acute or obtuse, can you find in the wrecked frame?

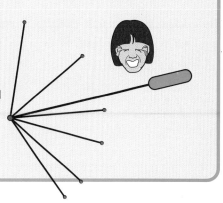

4 The Protractor

The protractor was invented to count how many degrees there are in an angle.

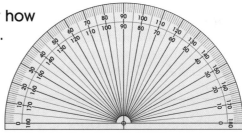

 A

1. Measure each of the following angles. Write your answer in the form ∠ ABC = 40°.

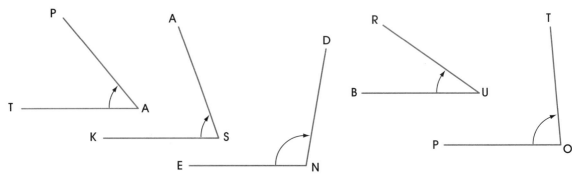

2. **a** Measure each of the following angles:

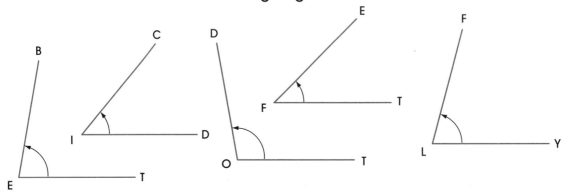

b Which angles are the same size as some of those in question 1?

3. Measure each angle. It may help to turn the book round. Put the shorter arm on the zero line.

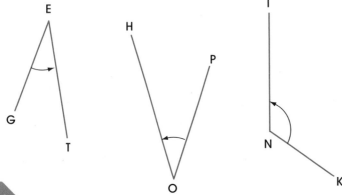
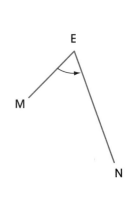

4. The smaller the angle is at the top of the tent, the faster it will get rid of rain.

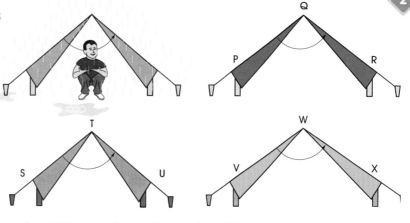

a Measure the size of: **i** ∠ PQR   **ii** ∠ STU   **iii** ∠ VWX

b Which tent is best for wet weather?

1. The side of the town hall is the five-sided shape ABCDE.

a Measure the size of:
   ❖ ∠ ABC   ❖ ∠ BCD
   ❖ ∠ BAE   ♣ ∠ AEG

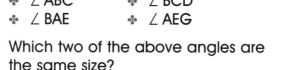

b Which two of the above angles are the same size?

c **i** Measure ∠ BAC and ∠ CAE.
   ii What is the connection between ∠ BAC, ∠ CAE and ∠ BAE?

2. When the penknife is open it makes ∠ ABC.

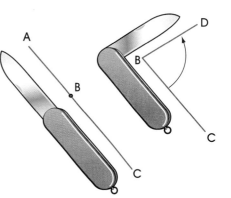

a What is the size of ∠ ABC?

b When it is partly closed it makes ∠ DBC.
   i Measure ∠ DBC.
   ii How many degrees did the blade turn through to go from BA to BD?

3. An artist is designing a stamp.

The rectangle ABCD represents the envelope.

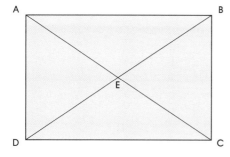

a Measure: **i** ∠ AEB   **ii** ∠ BEC

b What is the value of ∠ AEB + ∠ BEC?

c Measure: **i** ∠ BAC   **ii** ∠ DAC

d How many degrees in ∠ BAC + ∠ DAC?

e Measure: **i** ∠ BEC   **ii** ∠ ECB

f What can you say about ∠ BEC and ∠ ECB?

4. James wants to make stars for decoration.

To copy them he needs the angles at the points.

a 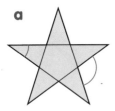   b   c 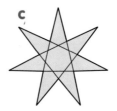   d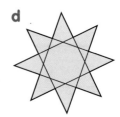

For each star, measure the angle:

♣ at a point   ♣ between the points.

5 ▷ Drawing Angles

Example   Draw PQR when PQ is 6 cm, QR is 5 cm and ∠ PQR = 55°

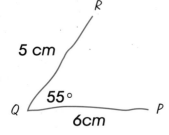

Q ————————————————— P

Draw PQ=6cm

Make a sketch – it will
help you plan your steps.

Set the vertex, Q, at the centre.
Set the arm PQ on the zero line.
Count round 55°. Mark it with a
pencil.

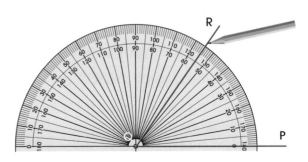

Draw QR through your mark, 5 cm long.

 A ————————————————————————————

1. Here are some rough sketches. Make accurate drawings of the angles.

a 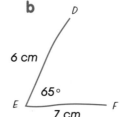   b   c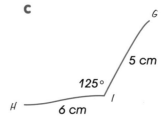

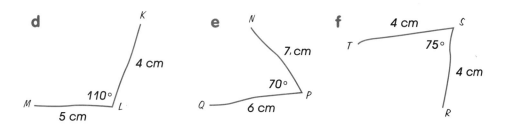

d

e

f

2. Draw the following angles. Decide for yourself how long you want the arms to be.

   a ∠ KLM 35°   **b** ∠ PQR = 100°   **c** ∠ TYH = 85°

3. **a** Draw a 6 cm line, PQ.

   b At P draw an angle of 60° where PQ is one arm.

   c At Q draw an angle of 60° where again PQ is one arm.

   d The two arms you have drawn will cross. Call this point R.

   e How long is: **i** PR   **ii** QR?

4. The picture of the Christmas tree is basically a triangle.

   a Draw a 10 cm line.

   b Draw two 55° angles which use this line as an arm.

   c Complete the triangle.

   d Measure the height of the triangle.

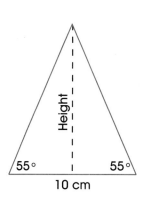

Challenge

Make an accurate drawing of this shape, where AB and PQ are running in the same direction.

Start with AB. Then draw the angles. You will need to use trial and error to find where the 1 cm line PQ belongs.

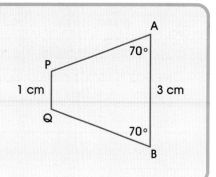

Unit 3

Information Handling

The Census – a giant snapshot of the whole nation

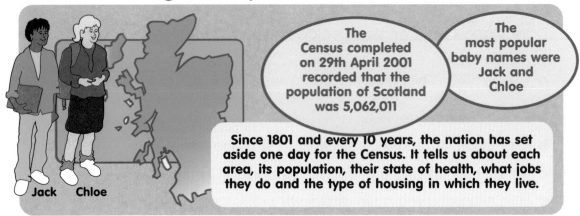

The Census completed on 29th April 2001 recorded that the population of Scotland was 5,062,011

The most popular baby names were Jack and Chloe

Since 1801 and every 10 years, the nation has set aside one day for the Census. It tells us about each area, its population, their state of health, what jobs they do and the type of housing in which they live.

Jack   Chloe

 1 **Looking Back**

Tally marks make counting easier.

Example   /// represents 3   ⁣𝖧𝖧𝖳 represents 5   𝖧𝖧𝖳 /// represents 8

1. How many children in your class enjoy maths? Copy and complete the table to record the results.

Vote	Count
Yes	
No	
Total	

2. Pupils in one class were asked to choose their favourite colour from a list of 4 colours.

   The results were:

red	red	blue	green	blue	purple	purple	green	blue	blue
red	blue	red	purple	blue	blue	purple	red	purple	blue
blue	green	red	red	blue	red	purple			

   Copy and complete the table using tally marks.

Colour	Tally	Count
Red		
Blue		
Green		
Purple		

3. Copy and complete the table to record the number of each of the different kinds of beads on the string.

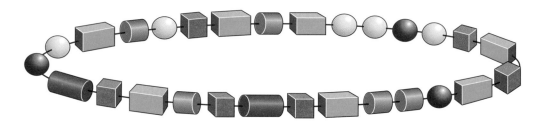

Type of bead	Tally	Number of beads
Green cuboid		
Red cube		
Blue cylinder		
Black sphere		
Yellow sphere		
Brown cylinder		

4. Primary 6 pupils were asked to give their opinion on new coconut flavour crisps. The results of the survey are shown on the bar graph below.

a   What opinion did most children give about the crisps?

b   How many children found them revolting?

c   How many children gave an opinion?

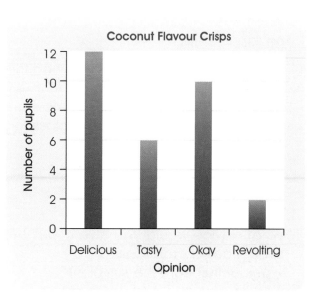

2 Become a Data Collector

A

Thirty days has September,
April, June and November.
All the rest have thirty-one,
Except February alone,
Which has twenty-eight days clear
And twenty-nine each leap year.

1. Make a list of the number of days in each of the months of the year. Use a calendar or the above rhyme to help you.

2. a Make a list of the people in your class with forenames containing the letter A.

   b Use the table below to help you explore the use of the letter E in the forenames of pupils in your class.

Number of Es	Tally	Number of forenames
0		
1		
2		
3		

3. Make a table to help you gather data about the people in your group. Include these details:
   boy/girl
   left-/right-handed
   hair colour.

4. The school wishes to provide a healthy option. More fruit ... fewer chips.
   They would like to find out the most and least popular fruits within your class.

   Copy and complete this short questionnaire, adding an extra 2 fruits to the list. Remember to include your own answers.

   What advice would you give if the school could order only two types of fruit from the suppliers?

	Do you like ...?		Favourite
Fruit	Yes	No	
Apples			
Grapes			
Bananas			
Grapefruit			
Oranges			

5. Primary 6 at Poppleburn Primary School made a questionnaire to use in a survey about their houses. This is an example of a completed form.

Type of house	Terraced	Semi-detached ✔	Detached	Flat	Other
Number of rooms	5 ✔	6	7	8	Other
Number of people living in house	2	3	4 ✔	5	Other
Number of windows	5	6	7	8	Other ✔
Colour of front door	White ✔	Brown	Blue	Red	Other

Please tick one box only in each row

a What type of house did the person live in?

b How many people were living in the house?

c What can you say about the number of windows in the house?

d ❖ Each person in your class should complete a blank questionnaire.
   ❖ Copy a blank questionnaire into your book. Use it to help you make a summary of your findings.

3 ▶ Organising Information

Sometimes data are grouped into class intervals to ease counting.

Example 1   A score falls in the interval 6–10 if it is 6, 7, 8, 9 or 10.
Example 2   A height falls in the interval 1·00 m – 1·99 m if it is any height between 1·00 m and 1·99 m including 1·00 m and 1·99 m.

1. This chart shows the amounts of each type of coin collected by the book stall in the first hour of the school fête. Copy and complete the table.

Value	Tally	Count	Money raised
1p	̶H̶H̶ ̶H̶H̶		
2p	̶H̶H̶ ̶H̶H̶		
5p	̶H̶H̶ ̶H̶H̶ /		
10p	̶H̶H̶ ̶H̶H̶ ̶H̶H̶		
20p	///		

23

2. A computer game has a 'High Scores' board. The best 8 scores are shown.

HIGH SCORES

Tom	2229	Mickey	7569
T.J	1596	Sal	9209
Kirsty	8029	Champ	5034
B.D.	1189	Pat	3087

a Copy and complete this table to help you organise the scores.

Class interval	Scores
0–3000	2229
3001–5999	
6000 and over	

b Arrange the scores into a list with the highest score first.

Challenge

Pat had another go and doubled her high score.
Copy the table again and complete it with the new top 8 high scores.
(Remember, Pat will now be on the 'High Scores' board twice.)

3. The school pupil council organise a stall.
They sell items at lunchtime to raise money for charity.
The number of items sold in the first week are shown below.

Items	Mon	Tues	Wed	Thurs	Fri
Bookmarks	5	6	5	8	4
School magazines	10	11	5	7	5
Pencils	3	8	6	5	6
Stickers	9	7	8	1	3
Totals					

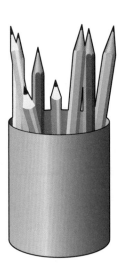

a Copy and complete the Totals row in your book.

b Draw a bar graph to show the total number of items sold each day.

c If they could only open 3 days in the week, on which days would you suggest they open?

B

1. Primary 7 at Poppleburn Primary school held a sponsored swimathon.
   The swimathon lasted for 2 hours. The class was split into 3 groups.
   Each pupil had to swim as many lengths as possible within the 2 hours.

   The number of lengths of the pool that each person managed is shown
   below.

   Group 1
   Ann 31; Peter 42; Sarah 16; Leanne 54; Enzo 10;
   Jason 18; Helen 50; Josh 12.

   Group 2
   Joanne 22; Rita 39; George 17; Steven 47;
   Alan 23; John 10; Mandy 61; Laura 27.

   Group 3
   Antony 15; Yvonne 49; Lynn 13; Kevin 45; Greg 63; Mark 34; Nisha 40;
   Jacqueline 14.

   a   Copy and complete columns 1 and 2 of the table to organise the data.

Group	Lengths swam		Total lengths swam	Total money raised
	Girls	Boys		
(1)				
(2)				
(3)				

   b   Each group will raise 50p for every length they swim.
       Complete the last column of the table.

   c   How much money did the class raise altogether?

2. Large areas of Scotland are mountainous. This is a list of the 10 highest
   mountains in Scotland. It gives each height to the nearest metre.

Height (m)	Name of mountain
1214	Ben Lawers
1221	Aonach Mor
1344	Ben Nevis
1291	Cairn Toul
1234	Aonach Beag
1309	Ben Macdui
1244	Cairngorm
1296	Braeriach
1258	Sgor an Lochain Uaine (Angel's Peak)
1220	Carn Mor Dearg

a Copy and complete this table.

Class interval (m)	Name of mountain	Height (m)
1201–1225		
1226–1250		
1251–1275		
1276–1300		
1301–1325		
1326–1350		

b A mountain higher than 914 metres is called a 'munro'.
What can be said about the 10 highest mountains in Scotland?

c Use the data to help you fill in the table below.

Class interval (m)	Tally	Number
1200–1219		
1220–1239		
1240–1259		
1260–1279		
1280–1299		
1300–1319		
1320–1339		
1340–1359		

d Which class interval contains the most data?

e Which of the class intervals contains no data?

◆ Investigate

What is the favourite snack item at break?

- ❖ Think of as many categories of items as you can ... fruit, crisps, sweets, etc.
- ❖ Try and keep the number of categories to about 5. Use 'Others' as a category if there is too great a variety of responses.
- ❖ Draw a table to record: the items, a tally, the total number choosing each item.
- ❖ Carry out the survey.
- ❖ Ask as many pupils as you can.

Unit 4 Decimals

Before 1971 the people of Britain used pounds, shillings and pence to buy things.

For three pounds and ten pence we could write £3 10p but more often we use a point to separate the pounds from the pence – £3·10.

Nowadays we just use pounds and pence.

Three pounds, seven shillings and six pence was written: £3 7s 6d

 Looking Back

1. Write each of the following using pounds, tenths and hundredths of a pound.

   a £5·32   b £12·08   c £8·70   d £23·01   e £0·05

2. Write the following amounts using the decimal point.
   a five pounds and twenty-five pence
   b thirteen pounds and two pence
   c twenty pounds and seven pence
   d one hundred pounds and a penny.

3. Martin and his mother went to the café for lunch. Starters cost them four pounds and seventeen pence. The main course cost six pounds and five pence. Ice cream cost three pounds.

   Copy and complete the bill. Use a calculator to total it up.

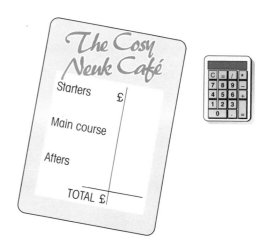

4. When Terri used his calculator to share £5 between two friends his answer looked like this:

   a What does it mean?

   b What would £6·70 look like on a calculator?

   c What would £2 and 5 pence look like on a calculator?

2 Decimal Numbers

Example

Here is a number line that shows the units broken into tenths.

> **The decimal point is used to separate the whole number part from the fractions.**
>
> **It sits between the unit digit and the tenths digit.**

Arrow **a** is pointing to 1 and 4 tenths ($1\frac{4}{10}$), which we can write as 1·4.
Arrow **b** is pointing to 0 and 6 tenths ($\frac{6}{10}$), which we can write as 0·6.

 A

1. Write in decimal form the number to which each arrow points.

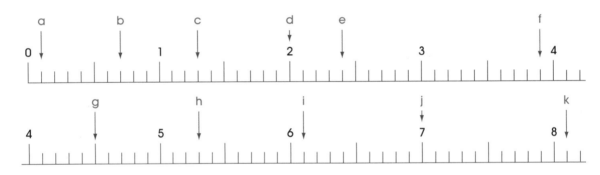

2. Make a copy of the number line from 0 to 4.

   a Use arrows to show the position of:
   ❖ 3·4   ❖ 1·8   ❖ 2·5   ❖ 0·6   ❖ 0·9

   b Use your drawing to help you put the numbers in order, lowest first.

3. Write each list of numbers in order, lowest first.

   a | 0·4 | 0·2 | 0·7 | 0·1 | 0·9 | 0·3 |

   b | 1·1 | 0·6 | 2·0 | 1·9 | 1·6 | 2·2 |

   c | 3·4 | 1·8 | 4·0 | 2·7 | 4·1 | 0·5 |

   d | 2·7 | 6·2 | 5·0 | 0·2 | 3·3 | 6·0 |

4. In the number 25·**3**, the **red** digit is worth 3 tenths ($\frac{3}{10}$). In a similar way, write the value of each **red** digit in the following numbers:

   a 32·**6**   **b** 40·**2**   **c** 86·**1**   **d** 100·**9**   **e** 223·**9**   **f** 525·**5**

5. Copy and complete each list of six numbers. Each follows a simple pattern.

   a 0·2, 0·3, 0·4, ☐, ☐, ☐

   b 3·9, 4·0, 4·1, ☐, ☐, ☐

   c 0·8, 0·9, ☐, ☐, 1·2, ☐

   d 1·3, 1·2, 1·1, ☐, ☐, ☐

   e 3·2, ☐, 3·0, ☐, ☐, 2·7

   f ☐, ☐, 3·9, 3·8, ☐, 3·6

3 Adding

Example

2·4 + 3·5 means 2 wholes and 4 tenths plus 3 wholes and 5 tenths.
This gives 5 wholes and 9 tenths which is 5·9.

```
   2·4
 + 3·5
 ─────
   5·9
```

Keeping the decimal points in a column makes sure you add wholes to wholes and tenths to tenths.

 A

1. Add the following pairs of numbers. Note the decimal points are kept in line.

   a 3·1
       + 3·2

   b 4·2
       + 3·5

   c 2·4
       + 0·3

   d 3·4
       + 2·6

   e 2·3
       + 4·8

   f 3·4
       + 2·9

   g 5·5
       + 2·7

   h 4·7
       + 0·6

2. Calculate:

   a 2·7 + 3·5 **b** 3·7 + 9·8 **c** 0·8 + 0·7 **d** 6·1 + 7·9 **e** 6·6 + 6·6

   f 0·6 + 6·0 **g** 12·6 + 3·1 **h** 45·2 + 81·8 **I** 56·8 + 99·9 **j** 23·8 + 56·2

3. Calculate mentally:

   a 0·1 + 0·3 **b** 0·6 + 0·2 **c** 0·3 + 0·4

   d 0·7 + 0·3 **e** 1·1 + 2·3 **f** 0·1 + 0·2 + 0·3

4. **a** At Sam's party 2·5 litres of lemonade and 1·5 litres of cola were drunk. How much in total was drunk?

   b At Tina's party 3·7 litres of cola and 2 litres of lemonade were drunk. How much was drunk in total at Tina's party?

5. A fashion designer needed 10·6 metres of fabric to make the bridesmaids' dresses. He needed 8·3 metres to make the bride's dress. What length of fabric was needed in total?

6. The DIY store has cut some lengths of wood.

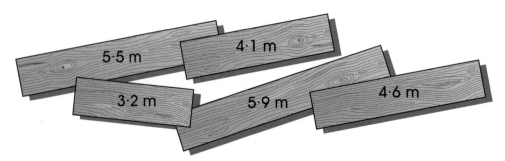

  a Which two pieces make a total length of 10 m?

  b Which three pieces make a total length of 16 m?

1. Calculate:

  a 2·4 + 3·2   b 1·8 + 4·6   c 5·7 + 2·3   d 12·3 + 8·9

  e 22·9 + 10·4   f 15·6 + 12·9   g 25·8 + 24·1   h 32·3 + 15·6

2. Add the following lengths together:

  a   22·9 m   b   33·4 m   c   45·7 m   d   55·7 m
      + 15·7 m   + 16·6 m   + 9·6 m   + 16·8 m

3. To decorate her room, Jasmine bought 2·5 litres of blue paint, 3 litres of white and 4·5 litres of grey.

  a How many litres of paint did she buy?

  b How many litres were not blue?

4. Mark and Mary Wilson and their parents went on holiday. Their bags had to be carefully weighed.

  a What is the total weight of the four bags?

  b Which two weigh about 21 kg?

  c Is the total weight of the females' bags heavier or lighter than the males' bags?

Mary Wilson 4·9 kg

Mark Wilson 8·2 kg

Mr Wilson 12·6 kg

Mrs Wilson 14 kg

Find the missing numbers in each case:

a 1·3 + □ = 1·9   **b** 2·1 + □ = 5·5   **c** 7·1 + □ = 9·0

Place the numbers 0·9, 6·6, 1·4, 2·0, 3·3, 5·3, 7·7 in this grid so that the total in each row is ten.

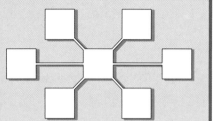

4 Subtraction

Example   Calculate   **a** 9·6 – 3·4   **b** 9·4 – 3·6

<table>
<tr><td>9·6</td><td>9·4</td></tr>
<tr><td>– 3·4</td><td>– 3·6</td></tr>
<tr><td>6·2</td><td>5·8</td></tr>
</table>

> Keep the decimal points in a line when subtracting.

1. Calculate:

a	6·7	b	9·6	c	4·4	d	8·7	e	7·2	f	5·4
	– 4·1		– 3·5		– 0·3		– 5·5		– 3·0		– 4·2

g	2·1	h	5·4	i	7·7	j	8·0	k	9·1	l	7·2
	– 0·6		– 1·7		– 2·8		– 3·7		– 6·9		– 3·8

2. Sam is looking at a couple of cars. The '4 by 4' is 3·8 m long. The saloon is 4·7 m long.

   How much longer is the saloon?

3. Peter is delivering some shopping. The parcel to his gran is 3·9 kg. The parcel to his mum is 8·1 kg. What is the difference in the weight of the parcels?

4. A water urn is filled with 9 litres of water.

   a At the interval 2·5 litres are used. How much is left in the urn?

   b At the lunch break a further 3·7 litres are used. What remains after the lunch break?

   c After the afternoon break it was found to contain just 1 litre. How much had been used during the break?

B

1. Calculate:

   a 23·7   b 34·8   c 55·1   d 62·3   e 80·0   f 61·1
      – 12·8   – 17·9   – 24·6   – 9·5   – 23·2   – 23·2

2. Work out the following differences:

   a 15·8 – 6·3   b 11·6 – 7·6   c 23·7 – 12·2   d 31·8 – 17·6

3. In the school javelin final, contestants threw the following distances:
   Jean 20·4 m   Asha 21·3 m   Fred 27·6 m   Tessa 30·6 m

   a What is the difference between the longest and the shortest throw?

   b How much further did Fred throw than Asha?

   c Before this competition Tessa's personal best had been 29·7 m. By how
       much did she beat it?

4. The model triceratops needed
   41·2 kg of clay to make it. This
   was 9·6 kg more than was
   needed for the model
   stegosaurus.

   a What weight was needed for the
       stegosaurus?

   b A T. Rex needed 3·8 kg less clay to make
       than the triceratops. How much clay is
       needed for the T. Rex?

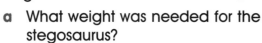

5. A water boiler holds 75 litres of water.

   a If 23·7 litres has been poured out, how much is left in the boiler?

   b Another 23·7 litres is poured out. How much is left now?

   c Can another 23·7 litres be poured out? Explain?

Challenge

Find the missing numbers:

   a 3·2 – ☐ = 2·4   b 9·5 – ☐ = 5·9   c 15·2 – ☐ = 7·2

5 Two Decimal Places – The Hundredths

A

1. Write in decimal form the number to which each arrow points.

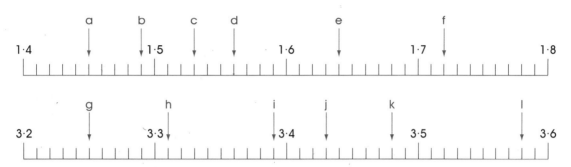

2. In the number 3·54 the **red** digit is worth 4 hundredths. In a similar way, give the value of the red digit in each of the following numbers:

   a 35·43   b 12·25   c 2·99   d 4·05   e 99·10   f 45·46

3. Calculate:

   a 79·34   b   45·08   c   44·69   d   23·21   e   65·60   f   41·27
     + 12·12   + 2·09   − 23·74   − 13·03   + 99·99   − 34·30

   g 60·09   h   50·11   i   92·91   j   9·02   k   88·08   l   9·70
     + 9·99   − 40·22   − 43·22   + 16·41   − 24·09   + 16·34

4. £2·45 means £2 and 45 pence; 5·19 m means 5 metres and 19 cm. Write the following in a similar way:

   a £8·67   b £12·80   c £23·05   d £88·00

   e 3·81 m   f 34·23 m   g 45·06 m   h 5·00 m

5. Frank has a 8·75 m plank of wood. He saws 6·19 m off.

   a How much is left?

   b Write it out in metres and centimetres.

6. Some friends had a competition to see who could grow the tallest sunflower. Here are the results:

   Tariq 1·67 m   Betty 1·89 m   Carol 1·76 m   Ewan 1·09 m

   a Who grew the tallest sunflower?

   b By how much did she beat her nearest rival?

   c What is the difference between the tallest and shortest flower?

   d If all the flowers were laid end to end, how long would they stretch?

Tariq

B

1. The pop group *Money Monet* have brought out their own merchandise. Their price list is shown opposite.

   What would the bill be for:

   a   a baseball cap and a mug

   b   a poster and a mug

   c   a scarf and a watch

   d   a T-shirt and a poster

   e   a T-shirt and a baseball cap?

They make the right impression!

Watch £15·89
Poster £4·25
Baseball cap £8·99

T-shirt £12·95
Scarf £11·27
Mug £4·78

2. *Money Monet*'s Double CD costs £21·88. If you paid for it without using notes, what is the smallest number of coins you would need?

3. At the Christmas Fayre, a fancy candle holder costs £9·50, a vase costs £11·35, a set of glasses costs £12·40 and a bowl costs £11·75. Which two of these items did I buy if I spent £21·25 exactly?

4. Stephanie bought a book for £5·75. What change would she receive from £10?

5. Four friends go shopping. They each take £20.

   John spent £19·25.   **Amy spent £12·40.**
   Sarita spent £11·80.   **Spike spent £15·95.**

   a   How much change did each person receive?

   b   How much more did John spend than Sarita?

6. Bill has a wonky table. The four legs have lengths:

   A 1·78 m   B 1·75 m   C 1·80 m   D 1·81 m

   a   What is the difference between the longest and shortest leg?

   b   Describe what would be cut from each leg to make the table level. (Assuming that you cut away the least amount that you have to.)

Challenge

Working with coins less than a pound only here is one way of having more than £1 but being unable to give change of £1.

What is the most amount of money I can have and not give change of a pound?

If we now permit the £1 coin to be used as well, what is the most I can have and be unable to give change of a £2 coin?

Unit 5 Time

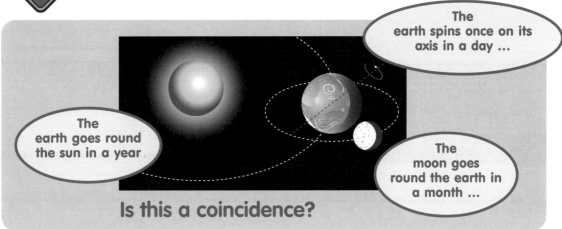

The earth spins once on its axis in a day ...

The earth goes round the sun in a year

The moon goes round the earth in a month ...

Is this a coincidence?

1 Looking Back

1. **a** Write down the circled date in three different ways.

   b On which day of the week is 21/11/05?

   c What date is the last Sunday in November 2005?

November 2005						
Sun	Mon	Tue	Wed	Thu	Fri	Sat
		1	2	3	4	5
6	7	8	9	10	11	12
13	14	15	16	17	18	19
20	21	22	23	24	25	26
27	28	29	30			

2. Match up each time with a display:

   Half past 3 in the afternoon.

   Quarter to 7 in the morning.

   Quarter to 7 in the evening.

   Half past 9 in the morning.

   Quarter past 6 in the evening.

   Quarter past 6 in the morning.

a (clock)

b `06:15 AM`

c `06:45 AM`

d (clock)

e (clock)

f `06:45 PM`

Channel 6

6.00 **A Place in the Sun** (T) (R)
6.30 **News and Sport**
7.05 *Film Michael* 1996
   John Travolta plays an angel
9.05 **Boys and Girls**
   Live game show

3. **a** How long is the film *Michael*?

   b For how many minutes does the news last?

   c Which programme is on for $\frac{1}{2}$ hour?

   d 'Boys and Girls' lasts for 65 minutes. When does it finish?

4. **a** How many days has June?

   b Name the eighth month.

   c Today is 30th April. What is tomorrow's date?

5. **a** Today is Monday 10th May. I go on holiday one week today. What date will that be?

   b I return on 24th May. How many days will I be away?

2 Units of Time

A

1. Change:

   a 3 minutes → ▇ seconds   **b** 5 minutes → ▇ seconds

   c 120 seconds → ▇ minutes   **d** 240 seconds → ▇ minutes

   e 10 minutes → ▇ seconds   **f** 30 seconds → ▇ minutes

   g $1\frac{1}{2}$ minutes → ▇ seconds   **h** $4\frac{1}{2}$ minutes → ▇ seconds

2. Change:

a 2 hours to minutes	**b** 3 hours to minutes
c 300 minutes to hours	**d** 420 minutes to hours
e 9 hours to minutes	**f** 90 minutes to hours
g $3\frac{1}{2}$ hours to minutes	**h** 600 minutes to hours

3. **a** Which is longer: 3h 12 minutes or 200 minutes?

   b What is the difference in time between the two?

4. The counter said that there were 286 minutes left on the video tape. John wanted to record $4\frac{1}{2}$ hours of programmes. Can he do this?

5. Change:

a 3 days to hours	**b** 48 hours to days	**c** 96 hours to days
d 10 days to hours	**e** 22 days to hours	**f** 36 hours to days

6. In Edinburgh last week it rained for $2\frac{1}{2}$ days. In Glasgow it only rained for 62 hours.

   a In which city did the rain last longest?

b How much longer?

7. Change:

   a 3 weeks to days b 28 days to weeks c 70 days to weeks

   d 8 weeks to days e 1 fortnight to days f 52 weeks to days

8. Change:

   a 2 years to months b 36 months to years c 3 years to months

   d 12 years to months e 6 months to years f 4 years to months

◆ **Investigate**

Terry thought, 'There are seven days in a week. There are four weeks in a month. There are twelve months in a year. So there are $7 \times 4 \times 12 = 336$ days in a year!!!'

Pat thought, 'There are 365 days in the year. What has happened to the 29 days?'

What is happening?

B

1. a My flight lasts 192 minutes. How many hours and minutes is this?

    b I will be away for 26 days. How many weeks and days is this?

    c I leave on a Wednesday. On what day of the week do I return?

    d My friend is away for a fortnight. How many more days am I away than she is?

2. One DVD records 22 hours of programmes.

    a How many episodes of *The Simpsons* can I record on one disk?

    b How much time would be left?

    c Can I record four episodes of *Star Trek* on one disk? Explain.

    d Calculate how many *TOTP 2* shows fit on one disk.

    e How much time would be left?

6.00 The Simpsons
6.20 TOTP2
      Bob Dylan Revisited
6.45 Star Trek: The Next
      Generation 1996
7.30 Meades Eats
      The contribution of Indian
      cuisine to British culture

◆ **Challenge**

Work out your age for this coming birthday – in seconds!!

3 Counting the Days

If I buy raffle tickets numbered 4 to 10, how many have I bought?

| 4 | 5 | 6 | 7 | 8 | 9 | 10 |

Now be honest. Did you say 6?

When we are counting numbered objects:

Subtract last from first … then add 1. $10 - 4 + 1 = 7$

A

1. In 2005 how many days are there from:

   a 3rd November to 27th November

   b 29th November to 3rd December

   c 22nd November to 6th December

   d 10th November to 24th December

   e 21st December to 8th January

   f 20th October to 16th November

   g 13th October to Christmas Day

   h 24th October to New Year's Day 2006?

November 2005						
Sun	Mon	Tue	Wed	Thu	Fri	Sat
		1	2	3	4	5
6	7	8	9	10	11	12
13	14	15	16	17	18	19
20	21	22	23	24	25	26
27	28	29	30			

December 2005						
Sun	Mon	Tue	Wed	Thu	Fri	Sat
				1	2	3
4	5	6	7	8	9	10
11	12	13	14	15	16	17
18	19	20	21	22	23	24
25	26	27	28	29	30	31

2. How many days is it from:

   a Mary's birthday to Duncan's birthday

   b Mark's birthday to Emma's birthday

   c Emma's birthday to Mary's birthday if it is not a leap year

   d Emma's birthday to Mary's birthday if it is a leap year?

The Birthday List	
Mary:	02 03 88
Duncan:	15 04 90
Mark:	27 01 92
Emma:	19 02 95

3. The Post Office has asked for suggestions for new sets of stamps. The table shows 12 suggested anniversaries.

Event	Date	Anniversary
A	Mar 4 1890	Forth Bridge opened
B	May 13 2000	Donald Dewer elected
C	July 11 1274	Robert the Bruce born
D	Jan 25 1759	Robert Burns born
E	Dec 28 1879	Tay Bridge disaster
F	Apr 6 1320	Declaration of Arbroath
G	Feb 8 1587	Mary Queen of Scots beheaded
H	Aug 17 1947	1st Edinburgh International Festival
I	Nov 5 1879	James Clerk Maxwell died
J	Oct 14 1969	50p coin issued
K	Sep 29 1996	Stone of Destiny returned to Scotland
L	June 17 1652	Great Fire of Glasgow

a Sort these 12 events into month order. Start with January and finish with December.

b Use this order to calculate the number of days from the anniversary of one event to the next.

Calculating leap years

A leap year has an extra day – the 29th of February. This diagram will help you decide if a year is a leap year.

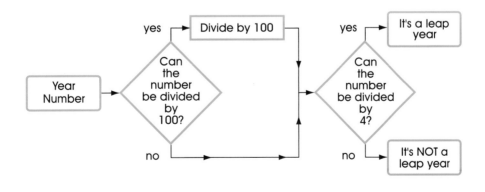

B

1. Use the diagram to help you decide which of these are leap years:

a 1600   b 1954   c 1844   d 2600

e 1900   f 2018   g 1984

2. Which events in Question 3 of Exercise 3a (see page 39) took place in a leap year?

3. The Olympic Games take place in leap years. Which of the following are Olympic Years?

   a 2003   b 2004   c 2038   d 2048

4. For soccer, the World Cup takes place two years after the Olympic Games. Which of the following are World Cup Years?

   a 2012   b 2014   c 2038   d 2054

5. Sort these holidays into order from shortest to longest. (Remember – in a leap year there are 29 days in February.)

   a From 16th February 1900 to 13th March 1900.

   b From 8th February 1992 to 1st March 1992.

   c From 23rd February 2006 to 19th March 2006.

   d From 14th February 2000 to 8th March 2000.

The 24-hour Clock

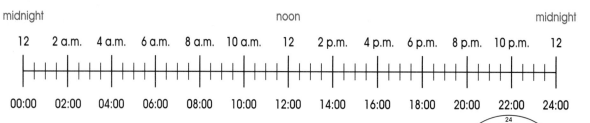

Example a 8.35 a.m. is written as 08:35
         b 8.35 p.m. is written as 20:35 – after 12 noon we add 12 hours to the time.

 A

1. Change each time into 24-hour time:

   a 12 noon   b 12 midnight   c 4 a.m.   d 4 p.m.

   e 8.30 p.m.   f 6.45 a.m.   g 11.40 p.m.   h 12.34 p.m.

   i 12.34 a.m.   j 10.03 p.m.   k 1.32 a.m.   l 12.01 a.m.

2. Change these 24-hour times into 12-hour times (remember to include a.m. or p.m.):

a `18:00` b `02:00` c `06:45` d `14:20` e `22:30`

f `00:00` g `24:00` h `12:00` i `00:56` j `15:05`

3. Match each time with a display:

Twenty past 2 in the afternoon

Quarter to 8 in the morning

Twenty to 7 in the evening

10 minutes before midnight

Half past 10 at night

Quarter past 11 at night

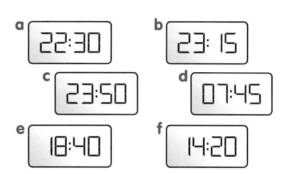

a `22:30` b `23:15`

c `23:50` d `07:45`

e `18:40` f `14:20`

4. Programming this old video recorder requires start and finish times in the 24-hour clock.

Write the correct start and finish times for:

a Charlie's Angels

b Lovejoy

c Are You Being Served?

d Beast

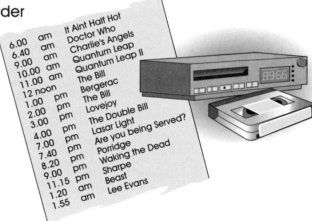

6.00	am	It Aint Half Hot
6.40	am	Doctor Who
9.00	am	Charlie's Angels
10.00	am	Quantum Leap
11.00	am	Quantum Leap II
12 noon		The Bill
1.00	pm	Bergerac
2.00	pm	The Bill
3.00	pm	Lovejoy
4.00	pm	The Double Bill
7.00	pm	Lasar Light
7.40	pm	Are you being Served?
8.20	pm	Porridge
9.00	pm	Waking the Dead
11.15	pm	Sharpe
1.20	am	Beast
1.55	am	Lee Evans

◆ **Investigate**

There have been attempts in history to make our time units metric.

Browse the Web for 'Metric Time'.

Find out about:

❖ $\frac{1}{10}$ of a day – the metric hour
❖ $\frac{1}{1000}$ of a day – the metric minute

How does a metric minute compare to our normal minute?

How would you arrange 10 months to the year?

5 Between Times

Example 1 A bus leaves at 8.40 a.m. and arrives at its destination at 11.30 a.m. How long was the journey?

Example 2 A bus leaves at 11.53 a.m. and arrives at its destination at 3.36 p.m. How long was the journey? When crossing noon, work with 24-hour times.

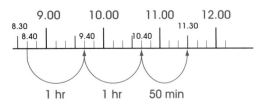

Answer: 2 hrs 50 min   Answer: 3 hrs 43 min

1. How long is it between each pair of times? Give your answers in hours and minutes.

a	12.10 p.m. to 1.20 p.m	**b**	8.30 a.m. to 11.45 a.m.
c	4.35 p.m. to 6.55 p.m.	**d**	06:10 to 09:55
e	16:43 to 18:45	**f**	6.24 p.m. to 10.34 p.m.
g	10:11 to 15:56	**h**	2.26 p.m. to 8.48 p.m.

2. Trains leave Edinburgh for Leuchars at the following times:

   Depart Edinburgh

   08:55 09:15 10:55 11:15 12:40 13:15 15:15 15:51 17:05 17:15 18:11 18:28 19:15 21:25 22:25

   a Write down the lengths of the gaps between trains throughout the day.
   b What is:
   ❖ the shortest gap between trains throughout the day?
   ❖ the longest gap between trains throughout the day?
   c I arrive at Edinburgh Station at 1.35 p.m. How long do I wait for a train to Leuchars?
   d Calculate the time between the first and the last train leaving.

3. Calculate the time from:

a	5.32 p.m. to 7.21 p.m.	**b**	10.30 a.m. to 11.12 a.m.
c	8.27 p.m. to 11.05 p.m.	**d**	01:47 to 03:20
e	18:36 to 21:07	**f**	3.38 p.m. to 8.32 p.m.
g	09:11 to 15:00	**h**	1.47 p.m. to 6.21 p.m.

1. Calculate:

   a the length of time spent on each subject

   b the time from the start of Language until Lunch

   c the length of the school day (from start of registration until the end of Art).

   d A local poet arrives at the start of Language and talks for $1\frac{1}{2}$ hours. How much time will be left for Mathematics when the talk finishes?

   e If the poet had come at the start of Music how much time would have been left for Art at the end of it?

The planned school day	
Registration	8.30 – 8.40 am
Language	8.40 – 9.30 am
Mathematics	9.30 – 10.20 am
Break	10.20 – 10.35 am
Env. Studies	10.35 – 11.25 am
R.E.	11.25 – 12.20 pm
Lunch	12.20 – 1.20 pm
Music	1.25 – 2.20 pm
Art	2.20 – 3.15 pm

2. The timetable shows the progress of a train from Inverness to London.

   a After the train leaves Inverness, how many stops does it make in the first $1\frac{1}{2}$ hours?

   b How long does it take to reach Perth?

   c From Perth to Preston takes how long?

   d What is the length of the whole journey?

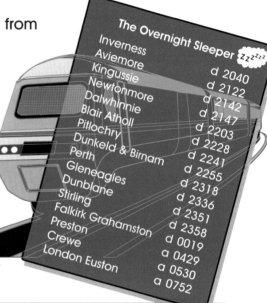

The Overnight Sleeper Zzzᶻᶻᶻ

Inverness	
Aviemore	d 2040
Kingussie	d 2122
Newtonmore	d 2142
Dalwhinnie	d 2147
Blair Atholl	d 2203
Pitlochry	d 2228
Dunkeld & Birnam	d 2241
Perth	d 2255
Gleneagles	d 2318
Dunblane	d 2336
Stirling	d 2351
Falkirk Grahamston	d 2358
Preston	d 0019
Crewe	a 0429
London Euston	a 0530
	a 0752

Challenge

Adam, Betty, Claire and Duncan want to catch the 13:14 to Bannockburn. It is 11:20 and they have to get to the station. They just have one tandem bike between all four of them. Adam can get the tandem to the station in 10 minutes, Betty in 20 minutes, Claire in 35 minutes and Duncan in 40 minutes. When two take the tandem they do the journey in the time of the slower person.

Make out a timetable to get all four to the station in time to catch the 13:14 to Bannockburn.

No trick answers – nobody walked!

Position and Movement

Hello Dad. Can you give me a lift home?

Describe where you are and I'll come and collect you.

1 Looking Back

1. The map shows where to find the different parts of Happy Valley Holiday Park. The parking is to the west of the restaurant.

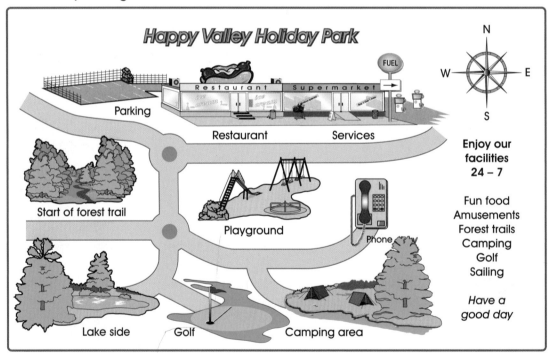

Happy Valley Holiday Park

Parking
Restaurant
Services
Start of forest trail
Playground
Phone
Lake side
Golf
Camping area

FUEL

N W E S

Enjoy our facilities 24 – 7

Fun food
Amusements
Forest trails
Camping
Golf
Sailing

Have a good day

a What is west of the golf course?   b What is east of the playground?

c What is north of the phones?

d James is at the camping area and wants to make a phone call. In what direction should he walk?

e Name the two features south of the restaurant.

f What is east of the lake and south of the services?

g Peter walked south and Sameera walked north. They met at the start of the forest trail. From where did each person come?

2.

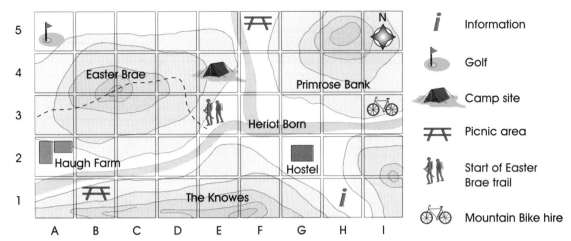

This map shows Easter Brae Countryside Estate. The grid helps us to describe position.

a There is a picnic area in B1. Where else is there a picnic area?

b In which square would you find:
   i the hostel   **ii** the golf course   **iii** Haugh Farm?

c What feature is given in square:
   i E3   **ii** I3   **iii** H1?

d The summit of Easter Brae is shown in four squares. Which four?

3. Sandra follows the green route through the Monster Maze. Her instructions read:

Forward 3; right 90°; forward 1; left 90°; forward 3; right 90°; forward 1; left 90°; forward 1.

Describe the red route in a similar way.

2 And Another Point ...

Midway between:

1 North and East we call north-east (NE)
2 North and West we call north-west (NW)
3 South and East we call south-east (SE)
4 South and West we call south-west (SW).

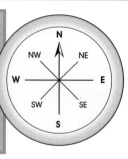

We can give more directions their own name to improve our ability
to describe journeys.

A

1. The red route on this grid could be described
    by E, SE, NE, NE, E.

    In a similar way describe:

    a the blue route   b the green route.

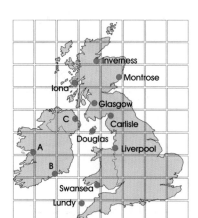

2. Which place is
    a SE of Inverness?
    b NW of Glasgow?
    c SW of Carlisle?
    d SE of Douglas?

    e NE of Lundy?

3. Three places are marked A, B and C. Galway is north-west of Cork. Belfast
    is north-east of Galway. State which place is represented by which letter.

4. The position of one chess piece can be described using another piece.
    The black bishop is west of the white knight.

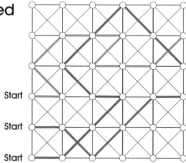

Using the white knight describe the
position of:
a the white castle
b the black knight
c the pawn
d the white bishop.

5. Use the empty red square to help you describe the position of:

    a the white castle   b the white knight
    c the pawn   d the black bishop.

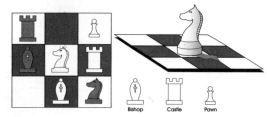

B

1. A is SE of 1 and S of 2.

   a Describe the position of B using 4 and 10.

   b Which letter is SW of 6 and E of 20?

   c Which letter is NE of 17 and NW of 11?

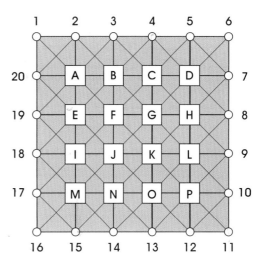

2. Which word is spelt out when you use the letters fitting these descriptions:

   a N of 12 and NW of 11

   b NE of 19

   c SE of 2 and SW of 8

   d N of 15 and SW of 4

3. **a** Jenny is facing north and makes a 90° clockwise turn. What way is she now facing?

   b Zoe is walking north-east and turns 90° clockwise. In which direction is she now facing?

   c Jack and Peter are back-to-back. Jack is facing south-east. In which direction is Peter facing?

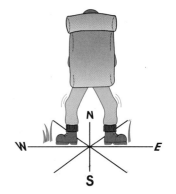

4. **a** A plane travelling due north changed its course to north-east. Through what angle did it turn?

   b A helicopter flying SW changed course to NE. Through what angle did it turn?

   c From a port one yacht heads off going NW. Another at the same time sets off south. What is the angle between their courses?

◆ Investigate

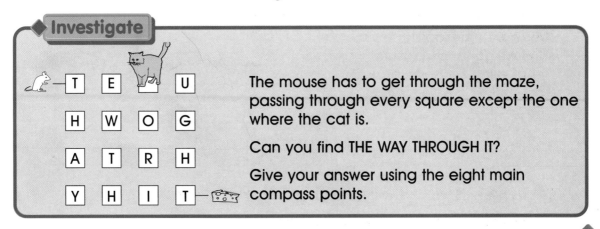

The mouse has to get through the maze, passing through every square except the one where the cat is.

Can you find THE WAY THROUGH IT?

Give your answer using the eight main compass points.

3 Bearings

If we want to be very accurate about describing direction we can use degrees.

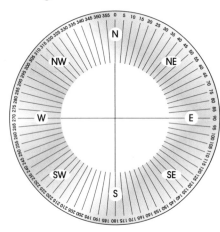

With 000° representing north, every other direction can be measured clockwise as shown on the protractor.

Note that every direction is represented by a three-digit number.

North-east is 045°

Example
The bearing of the plane from the airport is 110°

 A

1. Use a protractor to measure the bearing of each object from the lighthouse.

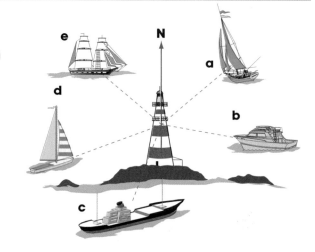

2. Travelling NE you are on a bearing of 045°.
   What is your bearing when you are travelling:

   a N   b E   c SE   d E   e SW   f W   g NW?

3. The map shows a journey made by a helicopter on a sightseeing tour. Measure the bearing for each part of the tour.

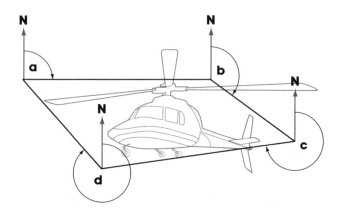

4 ▷ Properly Addressed

Describing the position of each point could be difficult.
But if you imagine they lie on a grid then you can give each an address.

The point A lies where the line labelled 1 across cuts the line labelled 5 up.
We say that A is the point (1,5).
The other points are B(2,3), C(4,4) and D(5,1).

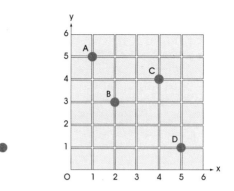

Each point is addressed by a pair of numbers:
The first number we call the **x-coordinate**.
The second number we call the **y-coordinate**.
When giving the coordinates of a point it is important to mention the x-coordinate first.

 A

1. Here is a poster for the sports club.

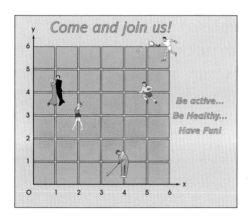

   What are the coordinates of:

   a the rugby player

   b the ballet dancer

   c the golfer

   d the dancing couple?

2. The captain's chart shows the positions of five other yachts in the race.

   a Give the coordinates of:
      i the Adele   ii the Eleanor
      iii the Bounty

   b Which yacht is at:
      i (1,2)   ii (4,2)?

   c Which two yachts have the same:
      i x-coordinate   ii y-coordinate?

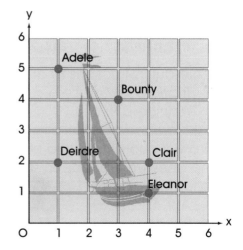

3. At the seaside Midge and his dad had a shot at the putting green. The grid shows the positions of some of the holes.

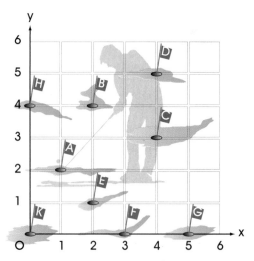

   a What are the coordinates of the holes labelled: i A ii B iii C?

   b Which hole has the same x-coordinate as: i C ii B?

   c The coordinates of F are (3,0). Notice the y-coordinate is 0. What are the coordinates of: i G ii H iii K?

   d Midge got a hole in one at E. He said it was E(1,2). Correct his mistake.

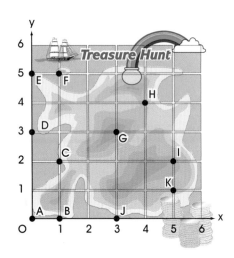

4. At the treasure hunt at the summer fête, people stick pins in a map where they think the treasure might be hidden. Henry thought it was at H(4,4).

   a Where did each of the following put their pin?
   ✤ Georgina   ✤ Iain
   ✤ Jenny   ✤ Colin

   b Andrew and Fiona thought it was buried at sea. What were their guesses?

   c Eric and Davina both tried to go as far west as they could. What do their guesses have in common?

   d Bunty and Jenny tried to go as far south as they could. What do their guesses have in common?

   e The treasure was found at (3,5). Who was closest?

5. We can draw the triangle PQR by plotting points and joining them as we go.

   The instructions look like:
   P(2,5)   Q(5,4)   R(1,2)

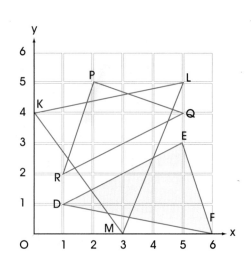

   Write out instructions to draw:
   a triangle KLM
   b triangle DEF.

6. Draw a coordinate grid numbered similar to the ones we have been using. Draw the following shapes:

   a A(0,4) → B(2,6) → C(4,4) → D(2,2)
   b E(3,5) → F(3,6) → G(6,6) → H(6,5)
   c C(4,4) → N(4,1) → P(6,2) → Q(4,0)
   d D(2,2) → N(4,1) → P(6,2) → Q(4,0)

A few names

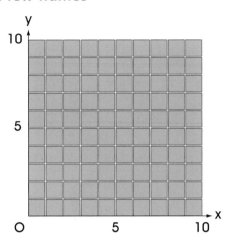

The line Ox is called the x-axis. The arrow points in the x-direction.

The line Oy is called the y-axis. The arrow points in the y-direction.

The point O has coordinates (0,0). It is called the origin.

 B

1. The coordinate grid has several points plotted on it.

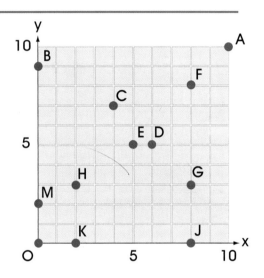

a O(0,0) lies on the x axis.
Give the coordinates of two other points that lie on the x-axis.
Copy and complete the sentence:
'**If a point lies on the x-axis its y-coordinate equals ...**'.

b O(0,0) also lies on the y-axis.
Give the coordinates of two other points which lie on the y-axis.
Copy and complete the sentence:

'**If a point lies on the y-axis its ... coordinate equals ...**'.

c The line joining H and G, HG, is parallel to which axis?

d To which axis is the line KH parallel?

2. A rectangle has vertices with coordinates A(1,2), B(7,2), C(7,6), D(?,?).

a Plot A, B and C on a coordinate grid.

b Find the point D and give its coordinates.

c Where is the middle of the side:
i AB ii AD?

d Draw the diagonals of the rectangle. Where do the diagonals cross?

3. Bryan's hobby is astronomy. He makes star charts. Here he has made a picture of the constellation, Orion the hunter. Some of the stars are named.

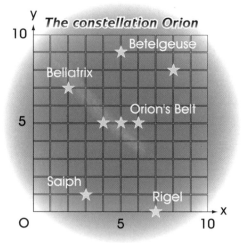

The constellation Orion

a Give the coordinates of:
   ✤ Betelgeuse
   ✤ Rigel
   ✤ Saiph.

b The three stars in a row are called 'Orion's Belt'. To which axis are they parallel?

c Bryan drew a line from the centre of the Belt to Betelgeuse. To which axis is it parallel?

4. One diagonal of the square PQRS has end points P(1,5) and R(5,5).

a To which axis is this diagonal parallel?

b Find the coordinates of the middle of this diagonal.

c Draw both diagonals. State the coordinates of Q and S.

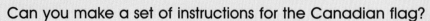

Challenge

Follow the drawing instructions to make the Scottish flag.

✤ Draw the rectangle (0,0), (0,6), (8,6), (8,0).

✤ Draw the triangle (1,6), (7,6), (4,4). Colour it blue.

✤ Draw the triangle (8,1), (5,3), (8,5). Colour it blue.

✤ Draw the triangle (0,1), (0,5), (3,3). Colour it blue.

✤ Draw the triangle (1,0), 7,0), 4,2). Colour it blue.

Can you make a set of instructions for the Canadian flag?

Unit 7 Fractions

"It was a game of two halves"

"Can I get the bigger half?"

1 Looking Back

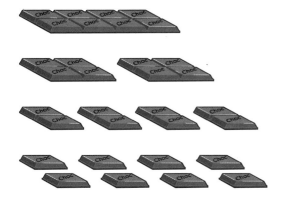

A whole bar of chocolate...

Two halves of a bar of chocolate ...

Four quarters of a bar of chocolate ...

Eight eighths of a bar of chocolate ...

1. One small piece of the chocolate bar is $\frac{1}{8}$ (one eighth) of the bar.

   a How many eighths do you get in $\frac{1}{2}$ (one half) of a bar?
   Complete the sentence '$\frac{1}{2} = \frac{?}{8}$'.

   b How many eighths do you get in $\frac{1}{4}$ (one quarter) of a bar?
   Complete the sentence '$\frac{1}{4} = \frac{?}{8}$'.

   c How many quarters to you get in $\frac{1}{2}$ (one half) of a bar?
   Complete the sentence '$\frac{1}{2} = \frac{?}{4}$'.

2. If ten pence is shared amongst 10 people, each receives $\frac{1}{10}$ of 10p.

   a What is $\frac{1}{10}$ of 10p?

   b If ten pence is shared amongst 5 people, each receives $\frac{1}{5}$ of 10p. What is $\frac{1}{5}$ of 10p?

   c How many tenths are needed to make one fifth?
   Complete the sentence '$\frac{1}{5} = \frac{?}{10}$'.

3. There are 30 days in September.

   a For one third ($\frac{1}{3}$) of the month there was rain. For how many days did it rain?

   b For one tenth ($\frac{1}{10}$) of the month Jenny visited her aunt. How many days is this?

   c For half of September she was on holiday. How many days' holiday did Jenny have?

   d How many tenths make a half?

4. Sixty minutes make one hour. How many minutes are in:

a half an hour	**b** quarter of an hour
c one fifth of an hour	**d** one tenth of an hour
e one third of an hour?	**f** What is half of half an hour?

5. What is the bigger amount in each pair?

   a $\frac{1}{5}$ of £90 or $\frac{1}{4}$ or £76.

   b $\frac{1}{3}$ of 66 metres or $\frac{1}{2}$ of 42 metres.

   c $\frac{1}{8}$ of 96 kg or $\frac{1}{5}$ of 60 kg.

2 Some More Fractions

10p is $\frac{1}{10}$ of £1
... a tenth part of £1
It takes 10 of them to make a pound.

20p is $\frac{1}{5}$ of £1
...a fifth part of £1
It takes 5 of them to make a pound.

5p is $\frac{1}{20}$ of £1
... a twentieth of £1
It takes 20 of them to make a pound.

2p is $\frac{1}{50}$ of £1
... a fiftieth of £1
It takes 50 of them to make a pound.

1p is $\frac{1}{100}$ of £1
... a hundredth of £1
100p = £1

 $\frac{3}{50}$ of £1

 $\frac{6}{100}$ of £1

Note that
$\frac{3}{50}$ of £1 = $\frac{6}{100}$ of £1

 A

1. What fraction of £1 is shown in each case?

 a b c d e

2.

is $\frac{1}{5}$ of £1   is $\frac{1}{5}$ of £2   is $\frac{1}{5}$ of £3

		i	ii	iii
a	How much is:	$\frac{1}{50}$ of £1	$\frac{1}{50}$ of £1	$\frac{1}{50}$ of £5.
b	Calculate:	$\frac{1}{100}$ of £1	$\frac{1}{100}$ of £2	$\frac{1}{100}$ of £12.
c	Find the value of:	$\frac{1}{20}$ of £1	$\frac{1}{20}$ of £10	$\frac{1}{20}$ of £15.

3.

is $\frac{1}{5}$ of £2

is $\frac{2}{5}$ of £2

is $\frac{3}{5}$ of £2

		i	ii	iii
a	Calculate:	$\frac{1}{10}$ of £2	$\frac{2}{10}$ of £2	$\frac{7}{10}$ of £2.
b	Calculate:	$\frac{1}{100}$ of £4	$\frac{7}{100}$ of £4	$\frac{23}{100}$ of £4.
c	Find the value of:	$\frac{11}{20}$ of £6	$\frac{7}{20}$ of £6	$\frac{11}{20}$ of £6.

4. Calculate:

		i	ii	iii
a	$\frac{1}{50}$ of:	£300	£650	£1000
b	$\frac{1}{20}$ of:	£80	£360	£1200
c	$\frac{1}{100}$ of:	£1200	£1700	£2900.

1. Peter wanted a skateboard. The cost was £42. His dad said that he would pay two-thirds of the cost if Peter found the rest.

   Calculate:

   a $\frac{1}{3}$ of £42   **b** $\frac{2}{3}$ of £42.

   c Complete the sentence: 'Peter paid £— and his father paid £—.'

2. Janine had 1500 marbles. $\frac{17}{100}$ of them are red. Calculate:
   a $\frac{1}{100}$ of 1500   **b** $\frac{17}{100}$ of 1500.

   $\frac{23}{50}$ of them are blue. Work out:
   c $\frac{1}{50}$ of 1500   **d** $\frac{23}{50}$ of 1500.

   $\frac{11}{20}$ of them are two-tone. Calculate:
   e $\frac{1}{20}$ of 1500   **f** $\frac{11}{20}$ of 1500.

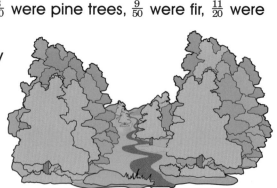

3. The lighthouse keeper logged 2400 vessels over the year.

   $\frac{31}{50}$ of these vessels were yachts. What is:

   a $\frac{1}{50}$ of 2400   **b** $\frac{31}{50}$ of 2400?

   $\frac{29}{100}$ of the sightings were made at a weekend. What is:

   c $\frac{1}{100}$ of 2400   **d** $\frac{29}{100}$ of 2400?

   $\frac{7}{20}$ of the vessels passed the lighthouse at night. What is:

   e $\frac{1}{20}$ of 2400   **f** $\frac{7}{20}$ of 2400?

4. There are 3500 trees in the forest. $\frac{23}{100}$ were pine trees, $\frac{9}{50}$ were fir, $\frac{11}{20}$ were birch and the rest were oak.

   a Calculate $\frac{1}{100}$ of 3500. How many pines are there?

   b Calculate $\frac{1}{50}$ of 3500. How many firs are there?

   c Calculate $\frac{1}{20}$ of 3500. How many pines are there?

   d How many oak trees are there?

3 Bits and Pieces

A

1. Find:

a $\frac{3}{5}$ of 150	**b** $\frac{2}{3}$ of 600	**c** $\frac{3}{4}$ of 44	**d** $\frac{7}{8}$ of 96
e $\frac{5}{8}$ of 400	**f** $\frac{3}{4}$ of 160	**g** $\frac{2}{3}$ of 123	**h** $\frac{4}{5}$ of 650
i $\frac{3}{8}$ of 168	**j** $\frac{1}{7}$ of 140	**k** $\frac{3}{7}$ of 700	**l** $\frac{5}{6}$ of 240
m $\frac{4}{9}$ of 981	**n** $\frac{5}{7}$ of 217	**o** $\frac{4}{7}$ of 2877	**p** $\frac{7}{8}$ of 2800

2. $\frac{3}{7}$ of the class are boys. There are 28 pupils in the class.

   a How many boys are in the class?

   b What fraction of the class are girls? How many girls are in the class?

3. $\frac{3}{5}$ of the traffic which passed the school between 9 a.m. and 10 a.m. were cars. 250 vehicles passed the school at this time.

   a How many cars passed?

   b What fraction of the traffic was not cars? How many vehicles is this?

4. A survey found that of the accidents that happen at home:

   $\frac{47}{100}$ **of them are falls**

   $\frac{12}{50}$ **of them are electrical**

   $\frac{3}{20}$ **of them are scalds or burns.**

   800 accidents are reported in the survey. How many were:

   a falls   **b** electrical   **c** scalds or burns?

   d Which is bigger $\frac{12}{50}$ or $\frac{3}{20}$?

B

1. A survey of 1700 people was done to find out the type of pets in the neighbourhood.

   The table gives the findings.

   a How many of the people asked had a:
   i cat   **ii** dog
   iii bird   **iv** fish?

   b The people asked had either one pet or no pets. How many people didn't have a pet?

Cats	$\frac{26}{100}$
Dogs	$\frac{21}{50}$
Birds	$\frac{3}{20}$
Fish	$\frac{1}{10}$

2. Camberwick Castle had 3000 visitors last month. They all signed the visitors' book.

$\frac{51}{100}$ were male

$\frac{13}{50}$ were American

$\frac{1}{10}$ were male American.

a How many: ❖ male ❖ female visitors were there?

b How many visitors were: ❖ American ❖ non-American?

c How many: ❖ male Americans ❖ female Americans were there?

d How many males were not American?

3. The astronaut brought 300 kg of rock back from the Moon.

$\frac{60}{100}$ of it was crystal
$\frac{39}{50}$ of it was black
$\frac{3}{10}$ of it was black crystal.

a What weight was:
   i crystal   ii not crystal?

b What weight was:
   i black   ii not black?

c What weight was:
   i black crystal   ii non-black crystal?

d What weight of the black rock was not crystal?

Challenge

Anna, Bill and Cathy's dad left £17, in pound coins, to be shared out amongst them.

He left instructions that Anna should get half, Bill should get a third and Cathy should get a ninth.

1. Use a calculator to check that the best that can be managed is Anna £8·50, Bill £5·66, Cathy £1·88.

2. Their mum, however, didn't have any pennies in change. She put another £1 coin in the pile making it £18.
   ❖ Anna got $\frac{1}{2}$ of £18 = £9 (more than she expected)
   ❖ Bill got $\frac{1}{3}$ of £18 = £6 (more than he expected)
   ❖ Cathy got $\frac{1}{9}$ of £18 = £2 (more than she expected)
   ❖ Now £9 + £6 + £2 = £17. So Mum got her £1 coin back.

   How can this be?

Equivalent Fractions

The pictures show the fractions of a pound, $\frac{1}{5}$, $\frac{2}{10}$, $\frac{4}{20}$, $\frac{10}{50}$ and $\frac{20}{100}$.

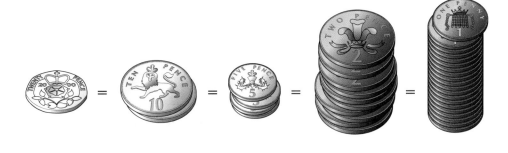

| $\frac{1}{5}$ of £1 | $\frac{2}{10}$ of £1 | $\frac{4}{20}$ of £1 | $\frac{10}{50}$ of £1 | $\frac{20}{100}$ of £1 |

They are called equivalent fractions – they are worth the same.

1. Looking at fractions of £1, find:

   a four fractions equivalent to i $\frac{2}{5}$ ii $\frac{3}{5}$ iii $\frac{4}{5}$

   b three fractions equivalent to i $\frac{1}{10}$ ii $\frac{3}{10}$ iii $\frac{7}{10}$ iv $\frac{9}{10}$

   c two fractions equivalent to i $\frac{2}{5}$ ii $\frac{4}{5}$

   d a fraction equivalent to i $\frac{1}{5}$ ii $\frac{3}{5}$

   e a fraction equivalent to i $\frac{1}{50}$ ii $\frac{9}{50}$ iii $\frac{21}{50}$ iv $\frac{43}{50}$

2. There are 120 hours in the working week (Monday to Friday). How many hours are the following fractions of 120 hours?

   a $\frac{1}{2}$ **b** $\frac{1}{4}$ **c** $\frac{1}{3}$ **d** $\frac{1}{5}$

   e $\frac{1}{8}$ **f** $\frac{1}{10}$

   g Discussing fractions of the working week, what do I mean when I say that $\frac{1}{5}$ is equivalent to $\frac{2}{10}$?

   h How many quarters are equivalent to $\frac{1}{2}$?

   i How many eighths are equivalent to $\frac{3}{4}$?

   j How many eighths are equivalent to $\frac{5}{10}$?

3. Find:

    a $\frac{3}{5}$ of 1000 m   **b** $\frac{5}{10}$ of 1000 m   **c** $\frac{12}{20}$ of 1000 m

    d $\frac{25}{50}$ of 1000 m

Give a fraction equivalent to:

    e $\frac{3}{5}$ **f** $\frac{5}{10}$

> Consider the fraction $\frac{3}{4}$. We can make a new fraction by multiplying
> top and bottom by 5: $\dfrac{3 \times 5 = 15}{4 \times 5 = 20}$

4. **a** Calculate: ❖ $\frac{3}{4}$ of 24   ❖ $\frac{15}{20}$ of 24. What do you notice?

    b Try multiplying top and bottom by 25: $\dfrac{3 \times 25 = 75}{4 \times 25 = 100}$

Calculate $\frac{75}{100}$ of 24 … and write about what you notice.

> Consider the fraction $\frac{2}{3}$. We can make a new fraction by multiplying
> top and bottom by 2: $\dfrac{2 \times 2 = 4}{3 \times 2 = 6}$

5. **a** Calculate: ❖ $\frac{2}{3}$ of 60   ❖ $\frac{4}{6}$ of 60. What do you notice?

    b Try multiplying top and bottom by 3: $\dfrac{2 \times 3 = 6}{3 \times 3 = 9}$

Calculate $\frac{6}{9}$ of 60 … and write about what you notice.

Finding equivalents

The last few examples have shown us that when we multiply
the top and bottom of a fraction by the same number a
second fraction is produced which is equivalent to the first.

Example 1   Find three fractions equivalent to $\frac{1}{4}$:

$$\frac{1}{4} = \frac{1 \times 2}{4 \times 2} = \frac{2}{8} \qquad \frac{1}{4} = \frac{1 \times 5}{4 \times 5} = \frac{5}{20} \qquad \frac{1}{4} = \frac{1 \times 25}{4 \times 25} = \frac{25}{100}$$

Example 2   Find the missing numbers $\frac{4}{5} = \frac{?}{20}$

$$\frac{4}{5} = \frac{4 \times 4}{5 \times 4} = \frac{16}{20} \quad \ldots \quad$$ spotting that we must multiply top and bottom by 4 to get
the 20.

B

1. Use the method above to find three fractions equivalent to:

   a $\dfrac{2}{5}$ b $\dfrac{3}{10}$ c $\dfrac{7}{20}$ d $\dfrac{5}{8}$

2. Find the missing numbers:

   a $\dfrac{3}{8} = \dfrac{\square}{40}$ b $\dfrac{11}{20} = \dfrac{\square}{100}$ c $\dfrac{3}{5} = \dfrac{\square}{50}$ d $\dfrac{23}{50} = \dfrac{\square}{100}$

   e $\dfrac{3}{10} = \dfrac{15}{\square}$ f $\dfrac{17}{20} = \dfrac{85}{\square}$ g $\dfrac{7}{8} = \dfrac{42}{\square}$ h $\dfrac{9}{50} = \dfrac{45}{\square}$

3. a Write the following fractions as tenths:

   i $\dfrac{1}{2}$ ii $\dfrac{2}{5}$ iii $\dfrac{3}{5}$ iv $\dfrac{4}{5}$

   b Remembering that $\dfrac{1}{10} = 0\cdot1$, write these fractions as decimals:

   i $\dfrac{1}{2}$ ii $\dfrac{2}{5}$ iii $\dfrac{3}{5}$ iv $\dfrac{4}{5}$ v $\dfrac{7}{10}$

4. a Write the following fractions as hundredths:

   i $\dfrac{1}{2}$ ii $\dfrac{24}{50}$ iii $\dfrac{3}{4}$ iv $\dfrac{1}{4}$

   v $\dfrac{3}{20}$ vi $\dfrac{24}{50}$ vii $\dfrac{17}{50}$ viii $\dfrac{19}{20}$

   b Remembering that $\dfrac{1}{100} = 0\cdot01$, and that $\dfrac{27}{100} = 0\cdot27$, write these fractions as decimals:

   i $\dfrac{1}{2}$ ii $\dfrac{24}{50}$ iii $\dfrac{3}{4}$ iv $\dfrac{1}{4}$ v $\dfrac{3}{20}$

   vi $\dfrac{24}{50}$ vii $\dfrac{17}{50}$ viii $\dfrac{19}{20}$ ix $\dfrac{19}{100}$ x $\dfrac{3}{100}$

   Challenge

   Simon was asked to add $\frac{1}{2}$ and $\frac{1}{4}$.

   1. Write both fractions as decimals.

   2. Add the decimals.

   3. Turn the decimal back into a fraction.

   4. Add the following fractions:
      a $\frac{3}{20} + \frac{17}{50}$ b $\frac{3}{5} + \frac{7}{20}$

Unit 8 Whole Numbers

A taxi carries four people.

Ten friends want to go from Ayr to Troon.

So they order two and a half taxis!

It is often important to know that we are dealing with whole numbers!

 Looking Back

Do questions 1–3 without written working.

1. a 7×6 b 5×8 c 4×9 d 8×7
    e $48 \div 8$ f $63 \div 7$ g $30 \div 6$ h $81 \div 9$
    i $80 \div 10$ j 84×10 k 140×10 l $650 \div 10$

2. Tommy paid 54 pence for six dice.
    What was the price of one die?

3. A bag of sand weighs 380 kilograms.
    What is the weight of ten bags of sand?

4. a 36×4 b 72×8 c $96 \div 6$ d $98 \div 7$
    e 80×7 f $95 \div 5$ g 79×6 h $96 \div 8$

5. What is the remainder in each of these divisions?

    a $17 \div 5$ b $28 \div 6$ c $37 \div 9$ d $60 \div 8$

6. Round these measurements to the nearest ten metres:

    a   62 metres   b   47 metres   c   35 metres

    d   268 metres   e   972 metres   f   815 metres

7. Seven tickets to a pop concert cost £91.
    What is the cost of each ticket?

8. 84 guests are invited to a wedding meal. Six guests can be seated at each table.
   How many tables are needed?

9. There are 96 cards in a pack of Beat the Champ playing cards.
   Each player has the same number of cards.

   How many cards does each player get, and how many cards are left over, if there are:

   a 4 players   b 5 players   c 6 players
   d 7 players   e 8 players   f 9 players?

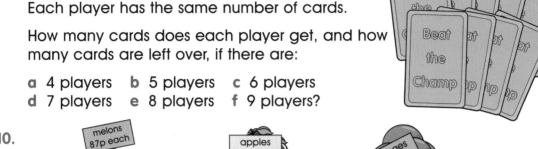

10.

   Calculate the cost of:

   a   half a dozen oranges   b   half a dozen apples   c   two melons
   d   What is the total cost of 9 apples, 7 oranges and 5 melons?
   e   How many apples can you buy for £1?
   f   How much more do eight oranges cost than eight apples?

2 Rounding

1.

| 0 | 10 | 20 | 30 | 40 | 50 | 60 | 70 | 80 | 90 | 100 | 110 | 120 | 130 | 140 |

   Round these numbers to the nearest ten. The number line may help.
   a 11   b 29   c 37   d 42   e 65   f 94
   g 98   h 116   i 153   j 188   k 706   l 825

2. Round these numbers to the nearest ten:
    a 1632   b 2417   c 3648   d 6906   e 8072   f 3335

3.

| 0 | 100 | 200 | 300 | 400 | 500 | 600 | 700 | 800 | 900 | 1000 | 1100 | 1200 | 1300 | 1400 |

   Round these numbers to the nearest hundred:
   a 178   b 329   c 463   d 770   e 849   f 950
   g 1120   h 1184   i 1270   j 1339   k 4627   l 7188

4. Round these lengths to the nearest metre:

a 7m 38cm b 12m 67cm c 19m 39cm

d 20m 72cm e 14m 9cm f 8m 50cm

> When we take measurements we often round off.

5. Round these weights to the nearest kilogram:

a 3kg 900g b 5kg 150g c 6kg 520g

d 7kg 500g e 8kg 95g f 2kg 8g

> We can estimate answers to calculations by rounding before we calculate.

6. Estimate each calculation by first rounding each measurement to the nearest ten metres.

   a 78 m × 6   b 53 m × 4   c 123 m × 5   d 688 m × 2

7. Estimate these calculations by first rounding to the nearest hundred metres.

   a 413 m × 3   b 726 m × 4   c 2672 m × 2   d 3450 m × 6

8. The table gives the names and heights of the highest mountains in four continents. Round each height to the nearest:

   a ten metres
   b hundred metres
   c thousand metres

	Mountain	Height
i	Mont Blanc (Europe)	4807 m
ii	Mount Everest (Asia)	8850 m
iii	Kilimanjaro (Africa)	5895 m
iv	Aconcagua (America)	6960 m

9. The five biggest crowds at football matches in Britain one Saturday were:

   67 208   58 906   43 541   36 038   34 801

   Round off each figure to the nearest:

   a ten   b hundred   c thousand

10. Give an estimate for each of these by first rounding each 3-digit number to the nearest hundred:

    a 264 + 538   b 891 − 408   c 419 × 7   d 893 ÷ 6

11. Estimate these by first rounding each 4-digit number to the nearest thousand:

    a 4874 × 8   b 6378 ÷ 5   c 9086 + 7188   d 5417 − 2378

B

1. Bubble Chews cost 4 pence each.
   How many can be bought for 30 pence?

2. A Youth Club has 45 members who want to play netball.
   There are seven players in a netball team.
   How many netball teams can be formed?

3. Tables in the dining hall seat six pupils. How many tables are needed to seat:

   a 50 pupils   b 80 pupils

4. Supa kites are made with four aluminium rods.
   How many Supa kites can be made with 25 rods?

5. A railway carriage can seat 60 passengers.
   How many carriages are needed to seat 200 passengers?

6. Paint is sold in $2\frac{1}{2}$ litre cans. 9 litres of green paint
   are needed to paint the Youth Club fence.

   a How many cans of green paint should be
     bought?
   b 14 litres of red paint are needed to paint the
     Youth Club walls. How many litres of red paint
     should be bought?

3 Multiplying

A

1. Find the answer to each of these by multiplying:

   a 375 kg + 375 kg + 375 kg + 375 kg + 375 kg

   b 625 cm + 625 cm + 625 cm + 625 cm + 625 cm + 625 cm
     + 625 cm + 625 cm

   c £8250 + £8250 + £8250 + £8250 + £8250 + £8250 + £8250

2. Find the answer:

   a 263   b 451   c 708   d 2061   e 3415   f 1926
     $\times$ 4 $\times$ 5 $\times$ 9 $\times$ 6 $\times$ 8 $\times$ 7

   g 842 × 7   h 1083 × 6   i 5726 × 8   j 3670 × 5

3. What number comes out of each function machine?

a IN   OUT   b IN   OUT
2634 x5   5817 x8

4. Which is bigger: a 7777 × 6 or 6666 × 7?   b 9999 × 4 or 4444 × 9?

5. What is the total weight of seven bags of cement each weighing 225 kilograms?

6. What is the total length of six pieces of rope each 948 centimetres long?

7. What is 4982 times 8?

4 Dividing

 A

1. Calculate:

   a 267 ÷ 3   b 850 ÷ 5   c 304 ÷ 4   d 693 ÷ 7   e 984 ÷ 8
   f 1284 ÷ 6   g 1926 ÷ 9   h 7865 ÷ 5   i 3696 ÷ 8   j 3724 ÷ 7

2. Calculate and find the remainder:

   a 819 ÷ 2   b 674 ÷ 4   c 316 ÷ 6   d 2643 ÷ 5   e 9651 ÷ 8

3. What number comes out of each function machine?

a IN   OUT   b IN   OUT
3108 ÷6   5944 ÷8

4. £838 is shared equally among seven friends.

   a How many whole £s does each friend get?
   b How much is left over?

5. How many bolts of length 9 centimetres can be cut from a metal rod 1125 centimetres long?

6. A garden centre has 5000 sunflower plants. It sells them in packs of 6.

   a How many packs of six are there?
   b How many sunflowers are left over?

7. A roll of wire 675 metres long is divided into eight equal lengths. How many whole metres are there in each length?

Challenge

1. Which number should appear in the IN circle?

IN   OUT

( ) ⟶ [×6] ⟶ [÷5] ⟶ (240)

2. Some numbers have been smudged.
   Work out the calculations and put in the hidden numbers.

   a
   ```
      6 3 ▨
        × 7
      ───────
      ▨ 8 4 5
   ```

   b
   ```
         3 3 ▨
      6 ) 1 9 ▨ 2
   ```

5   Making Use of Multiplication and Division

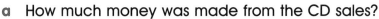

A

1. Nine friends win £1143 in a lottery.
   The money is shared equally. What is each friend's share?

2. *Purple Jelly's* latest CD 'Wobble Rock' was a flop.
   Only 768 copies were sold.

   a How much money was made from the CD sales?
   b Round your answer to the nearest £1000.

3. Sam's car can travel eight miles on one litre of petrol.
   He is driving 3176 miles to Spain and back.

   a How many litres of petrol will Sam need to buy?
   b Round your answer to the nearest ten litres.

4. Before a World Cup football match 3754
   Scotland flags were sold. How much money
   was made from the sale of the flags?

5. The table shows the number of visitors to the
   Magnum Leisure Centre one month.
   How much money was made from the sale
   of tickets for:

   a skating   b bowling
   c curling   d swimming

Magnum Leisure Centre		
Activity	Visitors	Ticket Price
Skating	7253	£7
Bowling	874	£6
Curling	3648	£8
Swimming	5196	£5

6. Round each answer in question **5** to the
   nearest £100.

7. Fame Academy has £1200 to spend on books.

   a How many maths books at £5 each could be bought?
   b How many science books at £9 each could be bought?
   c How many atlases at £7 each could be bought?

Challenge

| 25 | 9 | 4 | 7 | 6 | 8 |

The six cards above can be used to make the number 213
... $(25 \times 8) + 7 + 6 = 213$.

a Find two more ways to make 213.

There are some rules:
❖ all the cards need not be used
❖ if used, each card can be used only once
❖ you can add, subtract, multiply or divide.

b Can you make the number 456 from
   these cards?

Investigate

A sports shop buys 100 footballs.
Some of them cost £9 each and the rest cost £6 each.
Altogether the shopkeeper spends £801 on the footballs.

How many of each kind of football did the shopkeeper buy?

Unit 9 Letters as Numbers

Numbers ⟶ Letters as Numbers

How can I do ALGEBRA

There are no letters on my calculator!!

Here is one magic square:

6	1	8
7	5	3
2	9	4

Here is the recipe for lots of magic squares:

$x+1$	$x-4$	$x+3$
$x+2$	x	$x-2$
$x-3$	$x+4$	$x-1$

To see why, try $x=5$
then try: $x=6$, $x=7$…

1 Looking Back

1. Find the missing numbers:

a

3 7

total ?

b

4 ?

total 14

c

? 9

total 11

d

-4

? ——— 7

e

+3

? ———10———

f

-?

—12———17—

2. What number goes in each circle?

a ◯ + 2 = 9

b ◯ − 3 = 7

c ◯ × 3 = 18

d 7 × ◯ = 21

e ◯ ÷ 2 = 10

f 12 ÷ ◯ = 4

3. Find the missing numbers:

This is recorded as ③ × 5 points

a

◯ × 2 points

b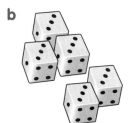

5 × ◯ points

c

◯ × 6 points

69

4. What does the letter stand for in each pair of cards?

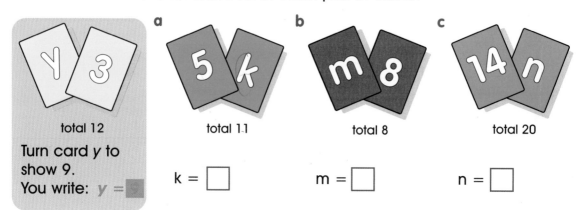

a total 11

b total 8

c total 20

Turn card y to show 9.
You write: y = 9

k = ☐

m = ☐

n = ☐

5. Replace each letter by the correct number:

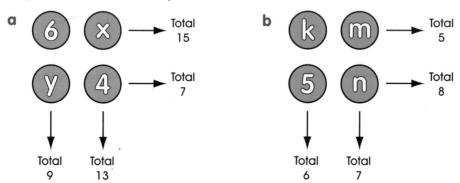

a
6 × x → Total 15

y 4 → Total 7

Total 9   Total 13

b
k m → Total 5

5 n → Total 8

Total 6   Total 7

2 Letters as Numbers

A

1. In these calendars the letters have values. For example, a = 2. Replace each letter by the correct number.

a

May 2006						
Sun	Mon	Tue	Wed	Thu	Fri	Sat
	1	a	3	4	5	b
7	8	9	10	11	c	13
d	15	16	17	18	19	20
21	22	e	24	25	26	27
28	29	30	f			

b

January 2009						
Sun	Mon	Tue	Wed	Thu	Fri	Sat
				1	2	n
4	5	m	7	8	p	10
11	r	13	14	15	16	17
s	19	20	t	22	23	24
25	26	27	28	29	30	31

2. Opposite pairs of numbers add up to the **total** given in the centre. Find the value of each letter. Write, for example $t = 8$

a

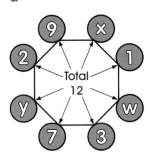

b

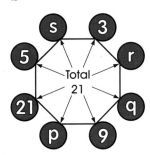

3. Find the value of each letter:

a

×	7	8	9	10
3	x	24	27	30
4	28	y	z	40
5	35	40	w	t
6	r	48	54	p

b

+	3	4	5	6
6	9	a	11	12
7	c	11	b	13
8	11	d	e	14
9	12	f	14	g

Challenge

If you move in the direction shown then follow the instructions for that direction.

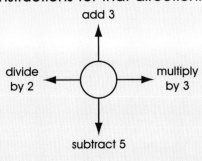

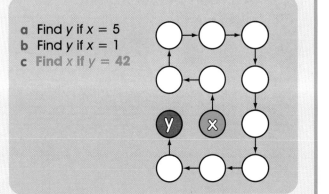

a Find y if $x = 5$
b Find y if $x = 1$
c Find x if $y = 42$

B

1. Find the values of the letters in each sequence:
   a 2, 4, 6, 8, *a*, 12, *b*, ...
   b 20, 18, 16, *m*, 12, *n*, ...
   c 1, *r*, 7, 10, 13, *s*, ...
   d 32, 29, *t*, 23, 20, *u*, ...
   e *c*, 7, 11, *d*, 19, 23, *e*, ...
   f *x*, 35, 29, 23, *y*, *z*, ...

2. Find the value of the letter in these card puzzles:

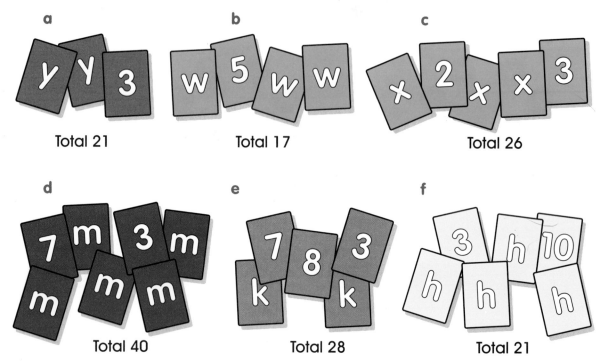

a

Total 21

b

Total 17

c

Total 26

d

Total 40

e

Total 28

f

Total 21

3. a   I am x years old. Alex is 3 years older than me. Our ages total 23 years.
        Find x.

    b   Diana is 12 years old. I am m years younger than her. Our ages total 19
        years. Find m.

    c   Chris and Graeme have a total age of 30 years. There is a difference
        of 5 years between them. Chris, the younger of the two, is y years old.
        Find y.

Challenge

Can you find the values of all the letters?

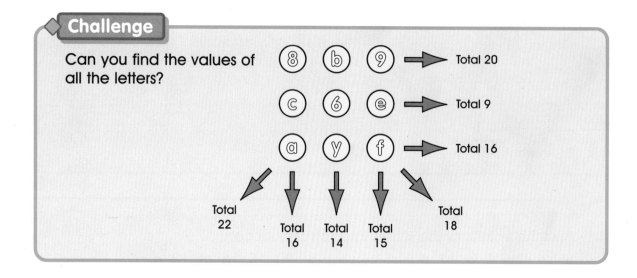

8 b 9 ⟶ Total 20

c 6 e ⟶ Total 9

a y f ⟶ Total 16

Total 22   Total 16   Total 14   Total 15   Total 18

3 Expressions

Bill is *x* years old. His wife is 5 years older than he is.
So she is *x* + 5 years old.

I have £*m* and spend £3.
So I now have £(*m* − 3)

Expressions have values but you need the value of the letter first!

If *m* = 7 then *m* − 3 = 7 − 3 = 4.

If *x* = 52 then *x* + 5 = 52 + 5 = 57.

m − 3 and *x* + 5
are called EXPRESSIONS

A

1. Find expressions for these:

   a   3 years younger than Meg

   b   6 years older than Tony

   c   1 year younger than Bert

   d   12 years older than Anne

   e   5 years older than Meg

   f   2 years younger than Tony

Meg
m years old

Tony
t years old

Anne
a years old

Bert
b years old

2. Find expressions suggested by:

   a   Bob spends £8   b   Iain finds £1
   c   Bob finds £2   d   Iain loses £3
   e   Bob earns £12   f   Iain wins £5

Bob has £*x*   Iain has £*y*

3. Find the value of:

   a   *x* + 7, when *x* = 3   b   10 + *y*, when *y* = 5   c   22 − *t*, when *t* = 7
   d   *m* + 1, when *m* = 2   e   7 + *q*, when *q* = 2   f   9 − *r*, when *r* = 3

4. If *y* = 7, find the value of:

   a   *y* − 6   b   *y* + 9   c   11 − *y*   d   *y* + *y*
   e   *y* + 4 + *y*   f   10 − *y* + 2   g   *y* − 1 + *y* − 2   h   7 − *y* + 5 + *y*

1. If $a = 3$ and $b = 5$, find the value of:

   a $a + b$ **b** $b - 3 + a$ **c** $13 - a - b$ **d** $1 + b + 4 + a$
   e $b - a$ **f** $5 + a - b$ **g** $a + a + a + a$ **h** $13 - a - a + b + b$

2.

   a If $x = 10$ find the ages of Alf, Tony and Jenna,
   b If $x = 12$ how many years older than Tony is Alf?
   c If $x = 16$ how much younger than Alf is Jenna?
   d Find the total of their three ages when $x = 13$.

   Alf is
   $x + 25$
   years old

   Tony is
   $25 - x$
   years old

   Jenna is
   $x + x + 3$
   years old

3. Copy and complete this Cross-Number Puzzle:

   $$m = 23 \quad n = 18 \quad k = 9 \quad t = 3 \quad w = 51$$

   Clues Across

   1 $m - 9 + m$
   3 $1 + k + k$
   4 $n + t$
   6 $m + w - 1$
   7 $m + k + w$
   9 $w - k + t$
   11 $w - 2 - k$
   12 $m - k$
   14 $n + k$
   15 $m + t + m$

   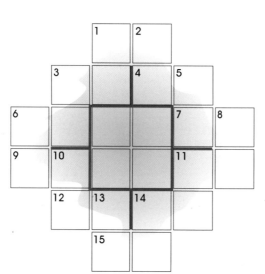

   Clues Down

   1 $n + 1 + n$
   2 $w + n + t$
   3 $k + t + 1$
   5 $k + k$
   6 $m + w$
   8 $n - k + n + t$
   10 $k + w - k$
   11 $1 + m + m$
   13 $m + n + t$
   14 $k - t + m$

Make the Magic Square that results when:

   a $x = 5$ **b** $x = 7$
   c $x = 12$ **d** $x = 105$

In each case calculate the 'Magic Sum', the total of each row, column and diagonal.

$x+1$	$x-4$	$x+3$
$x+2$	x	$x-2$
$x-3$	$x+4$	$x-1$

4 The Expressions are Multiplying

Here are five threes.
You write: 5×3

Here are six ys. You write: $6 \times y$ or $6y$

If $y = 7$ then $6y = 6 \times 7 = 42$
If $y = 5$ then $6y = 6 \times 5 = 30$

 A

Write an expression for each picture and find its value for each of the given values.

1.

a $n = 2$

b $n = 7$

c $n = 8$

2.

a $w = 5$

b $w = 11$

c $w = 20$

3.

a $e = 3$

b $e = 4$

c $e = 9$

4.
a $x = 9$

b $x = 15$

c $x = 25$

5. Find the value of:

a $4x$ if $x = 5$ b $3y$ if $y = 7$ c $8m$ if $m = 9$ d $\frac{1}{2}n$ if $n = 10$

e $2t$ if $t = 3$ f $9y$ if $y = 6$ g $\frac{1}{4}x$ if $x = 12$ h $7k$ if $k = 11$

6. Find an expression for the cost of:

a   b   c

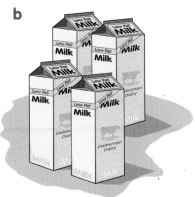

6 bunches at
x pence a bunch

4 cartons at
y pence a carton

3 tubs at
m pence a tub

7. Find the total shown on each set of cards:

a

b

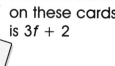
The total shown on these cards is $3f + 2$

c

d
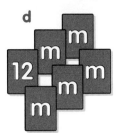

e
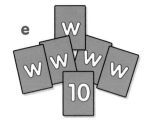

 B

If y = 6 then
$5y - 2 = 5 \times 6 - 2 = 30 - 2 = 28$

1. Find the value of:

a $3x - 4$ if $x = 2$ **b** $5y + 3$ if $y = 3$ **c** $\frac{1}{2}k + 3$ if $k = 10$
d $7r - 2$ if $r = 5$ **e** $4w - 11$ if $w = 3$ **f** $\frac{1}{3}m - 2$ if $m = 15$
g $12x + 3$ if $x = 0$ **h** $15y - 8$ if $y = 2$ **i** $4n + 7$ if $n = 9$

2. Complete this Cross-Number Puzzle:

$$x = 17 \quad y = 8 \quad w = 15 \quad t = 3$$

Clues Across

1	$7t - 3$
3	$4y - 3$
4	$5x + 8$
6	$2w + 9$
7	$5w + 1$
9	$3x - 3$
11	$2w - 6$
12	$3y - 3$
14	$2x + 4$
15	$5y + 3$

Clues Down

1	$5t - 2$
2	$6w - 1$
3	$3y + 5$
5	$10t + 7$
6	$4y + 2$
8	$4x - 4$
10	$25t + 7$
11	$2w - 2$
13	$4t + 2$
14	$4y + 1$

3. **a** If there are n kites how many full circles are there?
   b If there are m full circles how many kites are there?

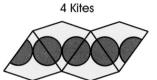

1 Kite   2 Kites   3 Kites   4 Kites

Unit 10 Information Handling

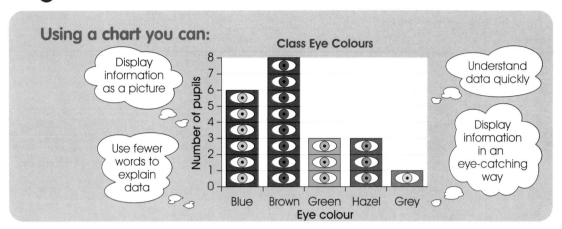
1 Looking Back

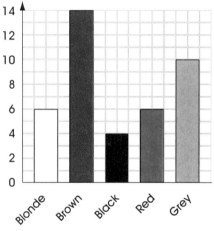

1. This bar chart or bar graph shows the result of asking a group of people about their hair colour.

   a Copy the bar graph into your jotter and add a title, and a label on both the x- and y-axes.

   b What was the most common hair colour?

   c How many people were surveyed?

2. The magazine sales for one week in the local newsagent were:

 11 copies   14 copies   17 copies   6 copies

   a Copy and complete the tables:

	Music Weekly	Hair & Make-up	Sporting News	Creative Computer	Total
Number Sold					
Money Taken					

   b Draw a bar graph to show the *number* of each type of magazine sold.

3. A survey on favourite pastimes was carried out with a Primary 6 and Primary 7 class. The results are shown here.

   a Copy and complete the table.
   b Draw a bar graph to display the results of the pastimes survey.

Pastime	Tally	Count
Sports	ＨＨ ＨＨ ＨＨ ＨＨ	
Watching TV	ＨＨ ＨＨ I	
Reading	ＨＨ ＨＨ	
Using a computer	ＨＨ ＨＨ ＨＨ II	
Listening to music	III	
Other	IIII	

   c Ask your class their favourite pastime and make a similar chart to compare your findings with those above.

4. A class of Primary 6 pupils recorded the weather outside their school for a week. The results are shown below:

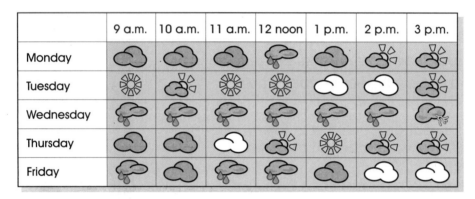

Key: Fine Thunder Rain   Sunny intervals   Sunny   Snow   Cloudy

   a Which day had the sunniest weather?
   b On which day did it thunder?
   c Which type of weather was not recorded?
   d Complete a table to show tallies and the total of each type of weather over the whole school week.
   e Draw a bar graph showing the total of each type of weather over the whole week.

2 Displaying Data – More Bar Graphs

It is often useful to make the bars on bar graphs horizontal. Here the types, or categories, are named on the y-axis.

A

Long jump champion

1. The Primary 7 championship final long jump competition results are shown below:

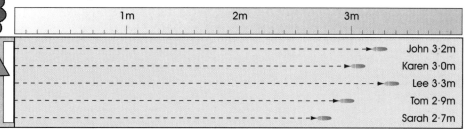

John 3·2m
Karen 3·0m
Lee 3·3m
Tom 2·9m
Sarah 2·7m

a Copy and complete this **horizontal** bar graph.
Notice in this case the bar is recording a *measurement* and not a *count*.

Long Jump results

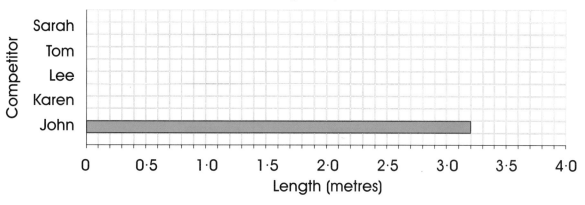

b Draw a results table with columns headed 'Place' and 'Name'.

2. The average annual rainfall for Scotland is shown on the map.

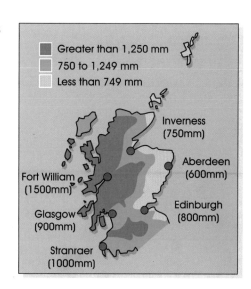

- Greater than 1,250 mm
- 750 to 1,249 mm
- Less than 749 mm

Inverness (750mm)
Aberdeen (600mm)
Fort William (1500mm)
Edinburgh (800mm)
Glasgow (900mm)
Stranraer (1000mm)

a Copy and complete the horizontal bar graph to display the average annual rainfall for the towns and cities shown on the map.
b Is the length of bar representing a *count* or a *measurement*?
c Which of the towns and cities shown is usually the wettest?
d Is a town which usually receives around 650 mm of rainfall likely to be on the East or West coast of Scotland?

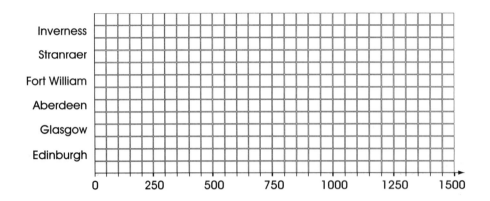

3. The national flags of 15 European countries and the dates when the flags were first introduced are given.

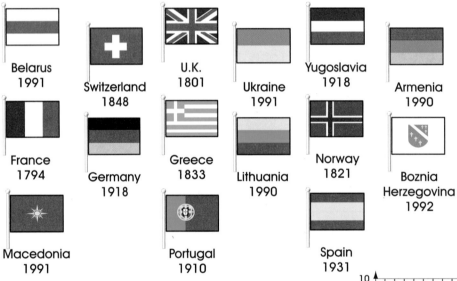

Belarus
1991

Switzerland
1848

U.K.
1801

Ukraine
1991

Yugoslavia
1918

Armenia
1990

France
1794

Germany
1918

Greece
1833

Lithuania
1990

Norway
1821

Boznia
Herzegovina
1992

Macedonia
1991

Portugal
1910

Spain
1931

a Make a bar graph using these scales to display when the flags shown were introduced.

b Is the bar representing a *count* or a *measurement*?

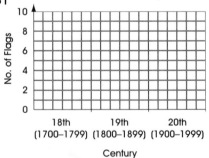

◆ Investigate

Draw a table or graph to find out:
1 What is the most common number of different colours used in the flags shown?
2 What is the colour most commonly used in the flags shown?

For a biology experiment a collection of dandelions have their heights measured in centimetres.

Note that the x-axis scale:

❖ is now in order, smallest to largest
❖ no size gets missed out – the gap at 8 cm means there were none in the sample
❖ we generally show the measurement either side of the sample (i.e. 5 cm and 10 cm).

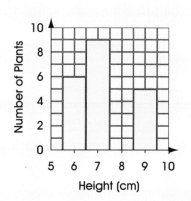

B

1. Samantha was collecting sea shells. She measured how wide each one was in centimetres:

3 4 4 5 5 6 4

4 3 4 5 5 5 5

4 4 3 5 3 4 3

6 3 3 4 5 3 5

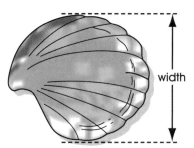

width

Make a diagram like the one above to illustrate her findings.
Let the x-axis show sizes from 2 cm to 7 cm.

2. Some apples in a batch were weighed in grams. The results are shown in the table.

Weight (grams)	25	26	27	28	29
Number	3	7	9	0	4

a Make a graph to show the results.
   Use an x-axis that is numbered from 24 to 30 grams.
b Can you work out the total weight of the batch?

3. To see if they were getting value for money, a market research team bought several ice lollies and measured their volumes in millilitres.

Volume (ml)	148	149	150	151	152
Number	5	2	8	7	1

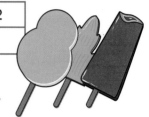

a Make a suitable diagram to show these figures.
A scale of 147 to 153 should be used on the x-axis.

b The wrapper for each lolly shows the volume on it.
Which figure do you think the wrapper should say?

3 Displaying Data – Frequency Polygons

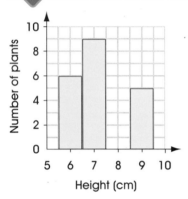

Instead of using this diagram …

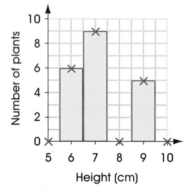

… mark off the midpoints of the tops of each bar, include the ends and zeros …

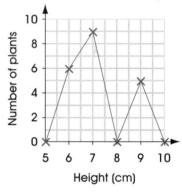

… and join them to form a **frequency polygon**. The bars are not needed.

1. Flight times were recorded on aircraft flying between Glasgow Airport and Geneva Airport in Switzerland.
The times were measured and rounded to the nearest quarter of an hour.

$1\frac{3}{4}$ 2   2 $2\frac{1}{4}$ 2 $1\frac{3}{4}$

2    $2\frac{1}{4}$ $1\frac{3}{4}$ 2 $2\frac{1}{2}$ 2

$2\frac{1}{2}$ 2   2 $1\frac{3}{4}$ 2 $2\frac{1}{4}$

a Copy and complete this **frequency polygon** to display the flight time data.

b What was the most common flight duration?

c Give one reason why the flight durations vary.

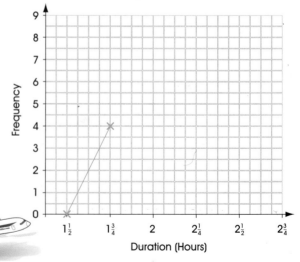

2. The pupils of Primary 6 each measured their reach.

150 cm	147 cm	148 cm	147 cm	149 cm	147 cm	154 cm
150 cm	151 cm	150 cm	146 cm	149 cm	151 cm	152 cm
149 cm	148 cm	148 cm	150 cm	149 cm	151 cm	150 cm
152 cm	150 cm	149 cm	147 cm	150 cm	149 cm	147 cm

a Sort the data by drawing a table with the headings 'Reach (cm)' and 'Frequency'.
b Draw a **frequency polygon** to display the data.

3. For a weather project the pupils measured the temperature outside, each hour, throughout a school week.

18°C	19°C	19°C	19°C	20°C	19°C	18°C
17°C	17°C	16°C	16°C	16°C	17°C	17°C
19°C	19°C	20°C	20°C	20°C	20°C	19°C
18°C	18°C	17°C	17°C	18°C	18°C	18°C
20°C	21°C	21°C	20°C	20°C	20°C	20°C

a Sort the data by making a table.
b Draw a **frequency polygon** to display the data.
c Do you think the pupils recorded these results in the summer or winter?

4   Grouping Information

Sometimes there are just too many values that the data can take to make a reasonable graph. We usually want between 5 and 10 categories to make a good graph.
What do we do if we are trying to record the heights of plants where every plant is a different height? One way is to group the data.

21	27	30	41	52
53	69	45	37	56
36	61	24	23	39
58	47	66	32	61

The heights of 20 plants in cm.

Group	Tally	Frequency
20–29	////	4
30–39	/////	5
40–49	///	3
50–59	////	4
60–69	////	4

The data grouped in tens.

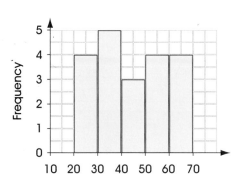

A meaningful graph can be drawn.

Unit
10

A

1. A survey was done on the lengths of 30 pupils' feet.
   The table below gives the findings in centimetres.

16	20	28	27	31	22	25	19	32	18
24	26	22	22	23	28	30	29	34	29
31	21	17	34	26	30	24	25	21	16

   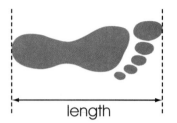

   length

   a Sort the data into the groups 15–19, 20–24,
   25–29, 30–34.

   b Use the groups to help you draw a suitable graph with bars to illustrate
   the findings.

   c Into which group did most pupils fall?

2. On the putting green, Malcolm measured the length of
   the last putt at each hole in centimetres.

8	33	16	23	37	28	41	36	18
12	26	7	40	15	6	12	11	29

   a Sort the data into the groups 0–9, 10–19, 20–29
   etc.

   b Draw a frequency polygon to display
   the data.

   c For which group of distances was he most
   successful?

3. Aberdeen Local Authority decided to use a large area of open ground to
   plant trees.
   The heights of the trees were measured one year after planting.
   The results are shown in this frequency table.

Height of Plant (cm)	20–29	30–39	40–49	50–59	60–69	70–79	80–89	90–99	100–109
Number of Plants	0	12	45	53	68	54	32	9	2

   a Draw a diagram like that above of the grouped data.

   b Draw a frequency polygon to display the data.

   c How many trees were measured?

   d How many of the trees measured were smaller than 40 cm?

B

1. The rainfall measured over the last 30 years at a weather station in Edinburgh gives these average monthly figures.

	Jan	Feb	Mar	Apr	May	Jun	Jul	Aug	Sep	Oct	Nov	Dec
Rainfall Amount (mm)	57.0	42.0	51.0	41.0	51.0	51.0	57.0	65.0	67.0	65.0	63.0	58.0
Days with Rain	12	9	11	8	10	8	9	10	11	12	12	11

a Draw a bar graph to display the average rainfall each month in Edinburgh.

b Which is the wettest month?

c Find the difference in millimetres between the wettest and driest months.

d Copy and complete this frequency table to show how many months have the same number of rainy days.

No. of Rainy Days	7	8	9	10	11	12	13
No. of Months	0	2					

e Draw a bar chart to illustrate the table.

f Copy and complete this frequency table using the data above.

Amount of Rain (mm)	40–44	45–49	50–54	55–59	60–64	65–69
Tally						
Number of Months						

g Draw a frequency polygon of the results in your frequency table.

2. A shopkeeper weighed out bags of mint humbugs weighing approximately 100 grams. The exact weights are shown below:

```
 94   101   97    97   104    99   102   101    98    99   100
100   103   96   101    94   101    96    99    97    92   103
102   100   99   104    96    98   104    93    94   100   105
 93    94   93   103   100    96    97   103   106    96    99
```

a Use a suitable graph to display this data (note that the data are measurements).

b Group the data with the aid of this table.

Weight (g)	91–93	94–96	97–99	100–102	103–105	106–108
Tally						
Number of Bags						

c Use this table to help you draw another of the same type of graph.

d Give a reason as to why the first graph is better.

Unit 11 Decimals

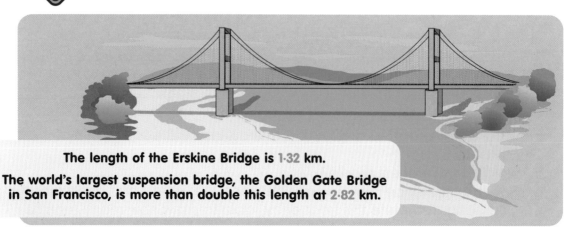

The length of the Erskine Bridge is 1·32 km.

The world's largest suspension bridge, the Golden Gate Bridge in San Francisco, is more than double this length at 2·82 km.

1 Looking Back

1. Round each of these numbers **to the nearest 10**.

a 127	b 382	c 617	d 593	e 214	f 396
g 97	h 125	i 955	j 41	k 3298	

2. Use rounding to help you estimate the answer to each of the following:

a 142 + 28	b 163 + 31	c 114 + 53	d 103 + 86
e 159 + 26	f 137 + 58	g 97 + 84	h 125 + 32
i 415 + 765	j 45 + 195	k 74 + 61	l 75 + 45

3. Calculate:

a 76 × 10	b 99 × 10	c 30 ÷ 10	d 136 × 10
e 200 ÷ 10	f 680 × 10		

2 Rounding

A

1. Round the following to the nearest whole number:

a 1·2	b 3·7	c 12·6	d 38·3	e 330·7	f 221·1
g 199·6	h 17·5	i 80·5	j 99·5	k 0·8	l 0·5
m 235·5	n 100·5	o 7·81	p 12·42	q 5·99	r 0·51

2. Round each length to the nearest centimetre:

a 2·3 cm	b 1·5 cm	c 6·8 cm	d 9·5 cm
e 19·6 cm	f 23·4 cm	g 30·8 cm	

3. Round the numbers in each sentence to the nearest 10:

    a There are 365·25 days in a year.
    b 899 pupils attended the assembly.
    c The fête collected £5135·75 for charity.
    d The farmer said there are 4840 square yards in an acre.
    e The planet Pluto is 3671 million miles from the sun.

4. Now round each number in question **3** to the nearest 100.

5. Round these numbers to the nearest whole number and estimate the answer to the calculation.

    a 2·4 + 3·2   **b** 1·8 + 4·6   **c** 15·5 + 2·3   **d** 12·3 + 8·9
    e 22·9 + 10·4   **f** 15·6 − 12·5   **g** 25·8 − 10·1   **h** 132·3 + 9·6
    i 13·91 + 11·24   **j** 29·33 − 19·91   **k** 6·56 − 1·04   **l** 7·81 + 3·5

6. A group of children made up harvest food parcels to give to the elderly. Four of the parcels weighed: **12·6 kg**   **13·7 kg**   **13·4 kg**   **11·3 kg**

    a Round each weight to the nearest kilogram.
    b Which two parcels had a combined weight of **about** 25 kg?
    c Which two parcels had a combined weight of **about** 27 kg?

Challenge 1

A decorator has five tins of emulsion for a painting job and needs about 18 litres of paint.

Which three tins should the decorator choose?

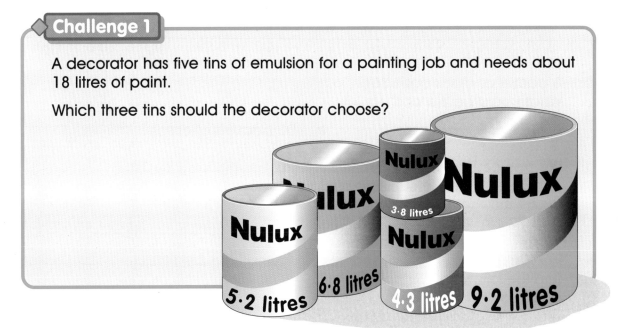

Challenge 2

Adam: "I'm going to walk between Arden and Bardry."
Fiona: "How far is that?"
Adam: "Oh! It's 12 km, to the nearest kilometre."

1. What is the least Adam can walk and still be telling the truth?

2. What is the most Adam might walk?

3. Fiona: "Well, I'm going to walk 20 km this weekend, measured to the nearest 10 kilometres!"

   a What is the least Fiona can walk and still be telling the truth?
   b What is the most Fiona might walk?

3 Multiplying and Dividing by 10 and 100

A

1. Calculate:

   a 3·2 × 10   b 6·5 × 10   c 0·21 × 10   d 16·38 × 10   e 5·06 × 10
   f 0·98 × 10   g 253·4 × 10   h 512·8 × 10   i 2·7 × 100   j 12·9 × 100
   k 1·31 × 100   l 9·96 × 100   m 21·3 × 100   n 0·92 × 100   o 10·6 × 100

2. A packet of crisps costs 35p.
   What would be the cost of:

   a 10 packets of crisps   b 100 packets of crisps

3. **We turn centimetres into millimetres by multiplying by 10.**
   Turn the following into millimetres:
   a 7·9 cm   b 9·5 cm   c 19·13 cm
   d 0·72 cm   e 194·4 cm   f 62 cm

4. **We turn pounds (£) into pennies by multiplying by 100.**
   Turn the following into pennies:
   a £3·45   b £17·08   c £94·50
   d £1·99   e £0·61   f £25·00

5. Calculate:

   a 56·0 ÷ 10   b 8·0 ÷ 10   c 121 ÷ 10   d 4·6 ÷ 10   e 9·7 ÷ 10
   f 10·9 ÷ 10   g 535 ÷ 10   h 606 ÷ 10   i 72·0 ÷ 100   j 6·0 ÷ 100

6. The weight of ten encyclopaedias is 14 kg. What is the weight of one encyclopaedia?

7. **We turn millimetres into centimetres by dividing by 10.**
   Turn the following into centimetres:

   a 12·4 mm   b 1254 mm   c 3 mm   d 14 mm   e 7·6 mm   f 1 mm

8. **We turn pennies into pounds (£) by dividing by 100.**
   Turn the following into pounds:

   a 375p   b 9211p   c 757p   d 8p   e 301p   f 79p

4 Multiplying by a 1-digit Number

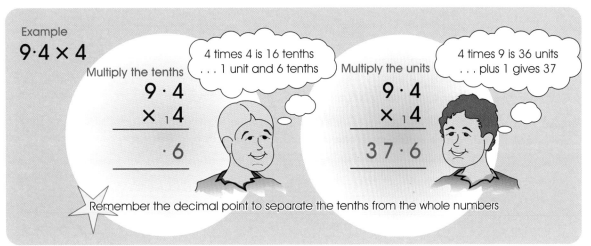

Example

$9·4 × 4$

Multiply the tenths

4 times 4 is 16 tenths . . . 1 unit and 6 tenths

```
  9 · 4
× ₁4
─────
    · 6
```

Multiply the units

4 times 9 is 36 units . . . plus 1 gives 37

```
  9 · 4
× ₁4
─────
3 7 · 6
```

Remember the decimal point to separate the tenths from the whole numbers

A

1. Find the answers to these:

   a   3·2   b   1·6   c   5·4   d   10·3
      × 3   × 6   × 5   × 8

   e   4·32   f   7·01   g   12·54   h   2·08
      ×   4   × 6   ×   2   ×   7

2. Calculate:

   a 4·2 × 4   b 3·4 × 2   c 12·6 × 3   d 20·6 × 5
   e 6·23 × 3   f 9·06 × 7   g 15·28 × 5   h 23·45 × 4

3. Ali bought six bottles of 1·5 litre Coola Cola for her birthday party.
   a How much cola is there in all six bottles of cola?
   b How much did she spend if each bottle cost £1·59?

4. The distance into town from Hayley's home is 4·76 km.
   She makes four return trips a week.
   a How many times does she cover the distance?
   b What is the total distance she travels in a week?

5. Calculate the cost of a game for:

    a four adults
    b three children
    c three adults and two children.

Price per game
Adults: £3·75
Children: £2·45

◆ **Investigate**

Consider the number 142 857

a When we multiply it by 2 we get 285 714.
   Look closely at the digits of the original number and the answer.
   What do you notice?
b Multiply 142 857 by 3. What do you notice?
c Multiply 142 857 by 4. What do you notice?
d Guess the answer to 142 857 × 5.
e Guess the answer to 142 857 × 6.
f You'll never guess the answer to 142 857 × 7!

B

1. Calculate:

    a 9·6 × 4   b 15·3 × 8   c 26·5 × 6   d 73·9 × 8   e 46·4 × 6
    f 3·25 × 5   g 9·63 × 7   h 19·34 × 9   i 30·96 × 6   j 59·07 × 8

2. A forklift truck lifts six crates.

    a What is the total weight the truck is lifting?
    b Round your answer to the nearest kilogram.

73·9 kg
73·9 kg
73·9 kg
73·9 kg
73·9 kg
73·9 kg

3. The distance around the Isle of Cumbrae is about
    16·49 km.
    Colin cycled this journey every day of his seven-day holiday.

    a What was the total distance he cycled?
    b Round your answer to the nearest kilometre.

4. A water urn contains 18·79 litres of water.
    An office block has one urn positioned in each of its eight floors.

    a   What is the combined volume of the eight urns?

    b   Round your answer to the nearest 10 litres.

5. Find the cost of:

    a   4 pairs of trainers

    b   7 CDs

    c   3 pairs of trainers and 5 footballs

    d   8 personal stereos and 4 CDs

    e   Calculate the cost of buying one of
        each to the nearest pound.

£13·99 each

£14·75 each

£69·75 a pair

£49·89 each

6. At the supermarket James saw that he could
    get one bottle of juice for £1·86. He saw that a
    six-pack costs £11·00.

    a   Is he better buying the six separately or as a pack?

    For each of the following decide whether it is better to buy separately or in
    bulk.

    b   A block of chocolate £2·17 each or a box of 8 for £17·50.

    c   A tin of biscuits for £3·26 or 3 tins for £10.

    d   A can of soup costs £0·97; a pack of 5 costs £4·80.

Challenge

Put the correct number in each box to complete the multiplications.

a
```
  ?·29
×    5
─────
41·?5
```

b
```
?3·62
×    7
─────
95·3?
```

c
```
 36·0?
×     8
──────
?88·72
```

5 Dividing by a 1-digit Number

A

1. Do these divisions:

   a $2 \overline{\smash{)}4{\cdot}8}$ b $3 \overline{\smash{)}6{\cdot}9}$ c $5 \overline{\smash{)}6{\cdot}5}$ d $3 \overline{\smash{)}5{\cdot}4}$

   e $5 \overline{\smash{)}6{\cdot}25}$ f $5 \overline{\smash{)}482{\cdot}6}$ g $7 \overline{\smash{)}4{\cdot}97}$ h $8 \overline{\smash{)}16{\cdot}24}$

2. Calculate:

   a $3{\cdot}6 \div 3$ b $6{\cdot}4 \div 2$ c $15{\cdot}6 \div 4$ d $249{\cdot}6 \div 3$ e $636{\cdot}6 \div 6$
   f $24{\cdot}88 \div 8$ g $15{\cdot}45 \div 5$ h $4{\cdot}64 \div 8$ i $20{\cdot}05 \div 5$ j $3{\cdot}28 \div 4$

3. Stewart buys four tickets for himself and his friends to see the latest adventure movie. If the total cost of the tickets is £15·80, what is the cost of one ticket?

4. The combined weight of a five-a-side football team is 267·5 kg.

   a What is the average weight of the players?
   b Round this answer to the nearest kilogram.

5.

   Big Softy Fabric Softener

   3 Litres £4·14   2 Litres £2·98

   a Calculate the cost of 1 kg of each type of potato.
   b Which is the better buy?
   c Calculate the cost of 1 litre of softener for each size.
   d Which is the better buy?

   Organic Potatoes

   5 kg £3·95   3 kg £2·52

Challenge

A group of five friends ordered some sandwiches for lunch. The total bill was £14·25. The friends share the bill equally.

a How much do they each pay?
b They pay with a £10 note and three £2 coins. How much change does each person get?

B

1. Calculate:

    a 96·4 ÷ 4   **b** 56·84 ÷ 7   **c** 36·24 ÷ 6   **d** 96·64 ÷ 8   **e** 380·7 ÷ 9
    f 24·56 ÷ 8   **g** 31·68 ÷ 4   **h** 85·96 ÷ 7   **i** 72·72 ÷ 9   **j** 48 ÷ 5

2. You can pay for this television by
    making six equal payments.

    a How much is one payment?
    b Mr Kelly has been allowed to pay
    for the television with nine equal
    payments instead. What is the
    size of Mr Kelly's payments?

Widescreen
Widescreen
£529·74

3. A supermarket splits 231·2 kg of
    potatoes equally into eight large sacks.

    a What is the weight of one sack of potatoes to the nearest kg?
    b At £10 a sack, what is the total cost of the potatoes?

4. Mrs Desai enjoys a relaxing bath every night before going to bed.
    Each week she uses in total 507·5 litres of water.
    What is the average volume of water she uses for each bath?

5.

Sunnyside Stables
Horse Riding
Lessons

6 lessons
£82·50

Contact:
Mr A. Trotter
Tel: 0101 345 678

Riverview Stables
Horse Riding
Lessons

8 lessons
£110·32

Contact:
Mr G. G. Gallop
Tel: 0101 777 888

Veronica would like to take a course of horse riding lessons.

a Which stable offers the best deal in riding lessons?
b How much cheaper is it per lesson?
c What would Sunnyside have to charge for its six lessons to be the same
as Riverview?

Challenge

Jamie works Monday to Saturday.
Each week he travels 262·56 km journeying to and from work.

a How many kilometres does he travel each day?
b What is the distance from his home to work?

Unit 12 Length

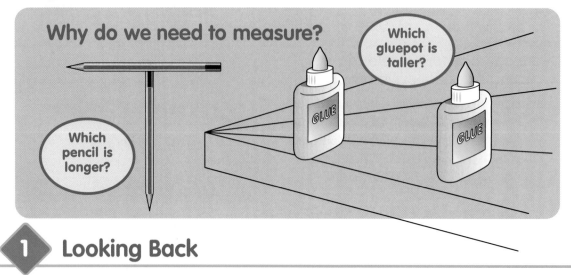

Why do we need to measure?

Which pencil is longer?

Which gluepot is taller?

1 Looking Back

To be good at estimating lengths, get to know yourself.
Use yourself as a ruler.

With your hand outstretched, measure from your **P**inkie to your **T**humb.
When you're next without a ruler, there's at least one length you'll know.

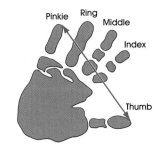

Pinkie Ring Middle Index Thumb

1. Copy and complete the table for your personal measurements:

Description	Length (cm)	Old-fashioned name
Thumb to Pinkie – hand outstretched		span
Width of thumb		inch
Tip of thumb to first knuckle		
Width of index finger		
Width of hand		hand
Tip of middle finger to elbow		cubit
Arm outstretched, tip of middle finger to nose		yard

2. Using only the personal measurements you have discovered, estimate the following lengths in centimetres:

    a   the width of the book   b   the length of your pen or pencil
    c   the width of the door   d   the height of your desk.

3. Now using a ruler, measure to see how close your estimates were.

4. Here is a typical set of instruments for measuring length.

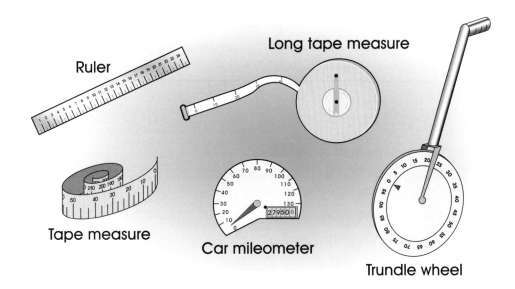

Ruler

Long tape measure

Tape measure

Car mileometer

Trundle wheel

Which one would you choose to measure:

a the length of a shoe b a person's height
c the length of a room d the length of your street
e the distance between
Edinburgh and Elgin?

5. Sarah noted the positions of four insects twice over five seconds.
By measuring the red lines, find how far each has travelled in the five seconds.

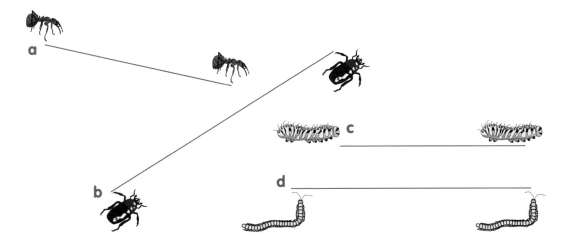

a

b

c

d

6. How many centimetres make:

a 1 metre   b $\frac{1}{2}$ metre   c $\frac{1}{4}$ metre   d $\frac{1}{10}$ metre

7. Name something in the classroom which you would estimate to be:

a 1 metre   b $\frac{1}{2}$ metre   c $\frac{1}{4}$ metre   d $\frac{1}{10}$ metre

2 Metric Length

A

1000 metres	=	1 kilometre
1 metre	=	100 centimetres
1 metre	=	1000 millimetres
1 centimetre	=	10 millimetres

1. Write each measurement in millimetres:

   a 2.5 cm   b 12 cm   c 0.6 cm   d 200 cm   e 12.34 cm

2. Write each of the following in metres:

   a 329 cm   b 4521 cm   c 60 cm   d 5281 cm   e 6 cm

3. Convert each length to metres:

   a 5000 mm   b 3297 mm   c 510 mm   d 300 mm   e 70 mm

4. Turn these distances into centimetres:

   a 34 m   b 2.7 m   c 0.85 m   d 0.05 m   e 1.06 m

5. How many kilometres are in each of the following?

   a 3497 m   b 5491 m   c 622 m   d 720 m   e 91 m

6. A doctor kept a chart of average heights on his wall.

   a Redraw the chart expressing the heights in metres.

   b How many metres difference are there between a 2-year-old and an 8-year-old boy?

   c Express the difference in height between an 8-year-old girl and an 8-year-old boy in metres.

Age	Boy	Girl
Birth	55 cm	55 cm
2	85 cm	83 cm
4	97 cm	103 cm
8	133 cm	127 cm
12	146 cm	152 cm
16	176 cm	165 cm
18	178 cm	165 cm

7. A caver's manual gives a list of the world's deepest caves.

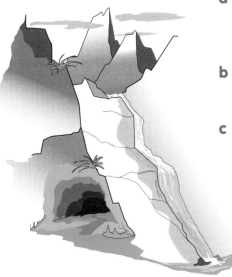

a Write the depth of the French cave and the deepest Spanish cave in metres.
b Write the depth of the Polish and Iranian caves in kilometres.
c What is the difference in depth between the Iranian and the French caves in:
❖ metres
❖ kilometres?

Location	Depth
Iran	750 m
Poland	784 m
Switzerland	830 m
Mexico	860 m
Austria	914 m
Russia	950 m
Italy	955 m
Spain	970 m
France	1·299 km
Spain	1·335 km

 B

1. a How much longer is 125 cm than 1·05 m?
b Which is bigger – 8·5 m or 805 cm – and by how much?
c What is the difference between 23·6 cm and 295 mm?
d Put the following list in order of size, largest first:
5 m, 495 cm, 5001 mm, 4·9 m, 4·09 m

When working with more than one measurement at a time ... make sure they use the same units.

2. a Mount Everest is 8·85 km high. Ben Nevis is 1344 m high. What is the difference between the heights of the two mountains? Kilimanjaro is 5·9 km, Elbrus is 5630 m, and McKinley is 6960 m high.
b List all five mountains in order, highest first.
c How much taller is Kilimanjaro than Ben Nevis? Give your answer in kilometres.
d How many kilometres taller than McKinley is Everest?

3. Before 1997, horses were measured in 'hands'. Now they are measured in centimetres. 10 cm = 1 hand.

a What is the difference in height between a horse of 15 hands and one of 157 cm?
b How many hands make a metre?
c Jane had a horse of 13·4 hands. Write its height in metres.

Investigate

Karen has found some measuring rods. She has 4 rods in total, which will allow her to measure every whole number length up to 40 cm.
She has a 1 cm rod and a 3 cm rod.
With these she can measure:

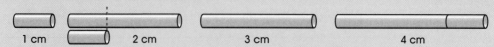

1 cm   2 cm   3 cm   4 cm

By including a 9 cm rod she can get up to 13 cm.

a   Show how each length up to 13 cm can be achieved.
b   What is the length of her fourth rod, needed to get to 40 cm?
c   Show how Karen could measure:
    ❖ 29 cm   ❖ 23 cm   ❖ 15 cm   ❖ 38 cm

3   Perimeter

The perimeter of a shape is the distance around it.

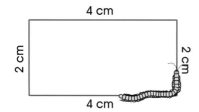

If the centipede wants to crawl all the way round the rectangle it will have to travel:

4 cm + 2 cm + 4 cm + 2 cm = 12 cm

The perimeter of the rectangle is 12 cm.

A

1.   Calculate the perimeter of each shape.

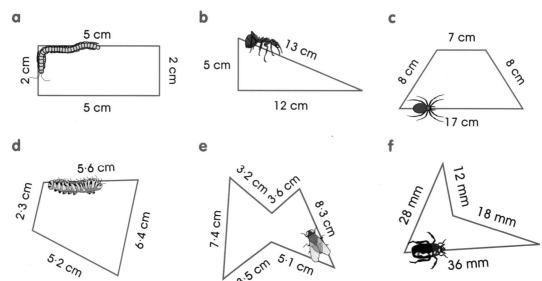

a
5 cm
2 cm
2 cm
5 cm

b
13 cm
5 cm
12 cm

c
7 cm
8 cm
8 cm
17 cm

d
5·6 cm
2·3 cm
6·4 cm
5·2 cm

e
3·2 cm   3·6 cm
7·4 cm
8·3 cm
3·5 cm   5·1 cm

f
12 mm
28 mm
18 mm
36 mm

2. A shape is *regular* if all its angles are the same size and all its sides are the same length.
   Calculate the perimeter of each of these *regular* shapes.

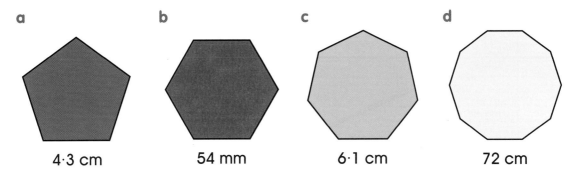

a   b   c   d

4·3 cm   54 mm   6·1 cm   72 cm

3. Measure the perimeter of each shape.

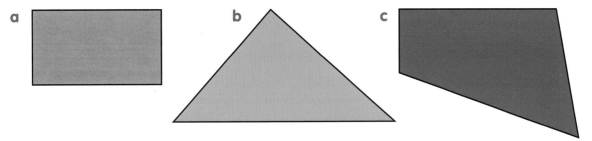

a   b   c

4. An estate is in a plot of land which is rectangular.
   The rectangle is 1890 m by 1750 m.

   Calculate the perimeter of the estate:
   a in metres   b   in kilometres.
   c A wire fence runs round the perimeter of the estate. A post every
      10 metres holds up the wire. How many posts are needed?

◆ Investigate

a Both A and B have the same
   perimeter. What is it?
b Count the number of squares
   inside each shape. Which has
   the bigger area?
c Experiment on squared paper
   to discover other shapes with
   the same perimeter but an
   even bigger area.
d What is the biggest area you can capture with this perimeter?

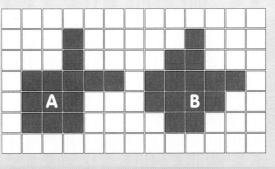

Where every angle is a right angle

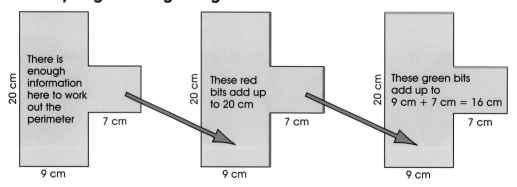

There is enough information here to work out the perimeter

These red bits add up to 20 cm

These green bits add up to 9 cm + 7 cm = 16 cm

Perimeter = 20 cm + **20 cm** + 9 cm + 7 cm + **16 cm** = 72 cm

1. Calculate the perimeter of each shape. Every angle is a right angle.

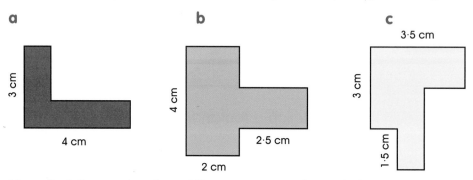

a   3 cm   4 cm

b   4 cm   2 cm   2·5 cm

c   3·5 cm   3 cm   1·5 cm

2. Now find the perimeter of these more awkward shapes.

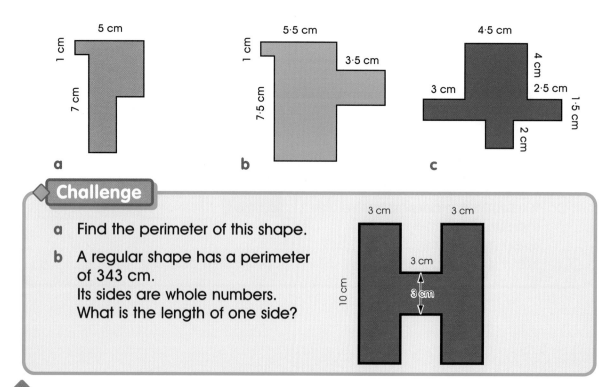

a   5 cm   1 cm   7 cm

b   5·5 cm   1 cm   3·5 cm   7·5 cm

c   4·5 cm   3 cm   4 cm   2·5 cm   1·5 cm   2 cm

Challenge

a Find the perimeter of this shape.

b A regular shape has a perimeter of 343 cm.
Its sides are whole numbers.
What is the length of one side?

3 cm   3 cm   3 cm   10 cm   3 cm

4 Problems in Length

A

> When working with more than one length … make sure to use the same units …

1. a Add 1·5 km to 650 m.
    b From 3·6 km subtract 900 m.
    c Add 3 mm to 27·6 cm.
    d Subtract 56 mm from 34·5 cm.
    e Divide 19·5 km by 3 and express your answer in metres.
    f Multiply 892 m by 7 and express your answer in kilometres.

2. A printers makes books of different sizes.
    The size they call 'Large' is 20·5 cm by 13·5 cm.
    What is the perimeter of this book?

    a when closed   b when open?

20·5 cm

13·5 cm

The 'Small' book is 10 mm shorter in both width and height.

    c What are the dimensions of the small book?
    d What is the difference in perimeters of the two books when closed?

3. Malcolm lived 2·9 km from school.
    Each day he cycled to and from school. He went home for lunch.

    a How far did Malcolm travel in one day?
    b How far did he travel in the school week?
    c One week he stayed with his gran who lives 1·6 km away from the school.
       How much less travelling did he need to do?

4. For charity, 12 people decide to do a marathon relay.
    The distance is 43 km. They each agree to run the same distance.

    Calculate, to the nearest metre, the amount each needs to run to cover the distance.

Challenge

Closer to the time of the race, three of the runners don't feel totally fit.
Everyone else agrees to run twice the distance of these three.
What distance, to the nearest metre, was covered by:
❖ the fit runners   ❖ the unfit runners?

Unit 13 Triangles

Tricycle   Tripod   Triplets

TRIANGLES AHEAD

1 Looking Back

1. Here are some shapes. Each is *regular* (its sides and angles are equal).

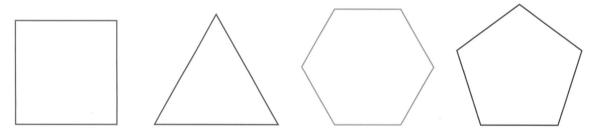

For each shape:

a How many sides has it?
c If the shape were to be cut out, how many ways could it be fitted back into the hole it leaves?

b How many angles?
d Draw each shape and mark on it a line of symmetry.

2. Look at the picture of this model house.

a Which parts of it are rectangular?
b Which parts are triangular?

3. Take a rectangular piece of
   paper and cut it in half along
   a diagonal.

   a What two shapes do you
     create?
   b How do you know the two
     shapes are identical?

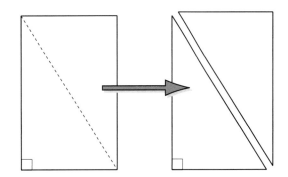

2 ► The Isosceles Triangle

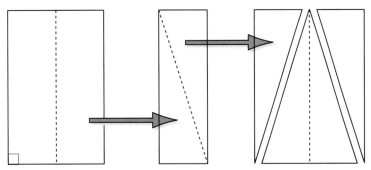

Fold a rectangle in half … and cut along one diagonal … three triangles are formed.

You have formed two right-angled triangles and one triangle with a line of
symmetry. Such a triangle is called *isosceles*.

A

---

1. Here the triangle has been labelled ABC.

   a Name the three sides.
   b Name the line of symmetry.
   c Name the two sides of equal length.
   d Name an angle equal to ∠ BAC.
   e What is the size of angle ∠ ADC?
   f What then is the size of ∠ ADB?

2. The two right-angled triangles can be fixed together to form another
   isosceles triangle. Let's call it PQR.

   a Name the line of symmetry
     of the triangle.
   b Name two sides that are equal.
   c Name two angles that are equal.
   d What size is angle ∠ PTQ?
   e What size is angle ∠ PTR?
   f If angle ∠ PRT = 70° what is the size of ∠ PRQ?

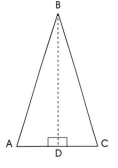

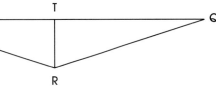

3. The word *isosceles* comes from the Greek *isosceles* (*iso* – equal and *skelos* – leg). Which of the following triangles are isosceles?

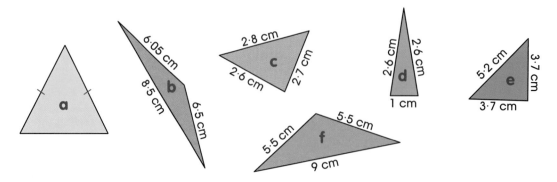

4. The symmetry tells us that an isosceles triangle has two angles equal.

   a Which of the following are isosceles?
   b Use a protractor to check your decisions.

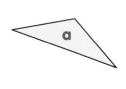 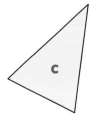 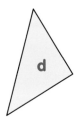 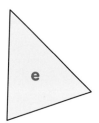

1. a Draw a coordinate grid on centimetre squared paper.
   b Plot the following points: A(2,1), B(3,4) and C(4,1).
   c Draw the triangle ABC.
   d What kind of triangle is ABC?
   e Name the equal sides.
   f The line of symmetry passes through the middle of the third side. What are the coordinates of this point?

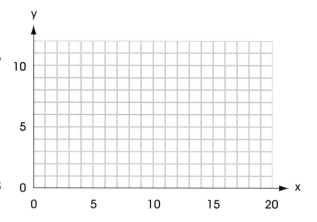

2. a   Measure the sides of triangle ABC you have drawn using a ruler.
    b   Copy this table and complete the first row for triangle ABC.

Triangle	Length of side	Length of side	Length of side	Perimeter
ABC	AB =	BC =	AC =	
EFG				
HIJ				
KLM				

Draw each of the following triangles on the grid and measure their sides with a ruler. Enter your results in the table.
    c   Triangle EFG with vertices E(6,1), F(8,7), G(10,1)
    d   Triangle HIJ with vertices H(2,8), I(5,10), J(8,8)
    e   Triangle KLM with vertices K(11,7), L(15,1), M(9,5)
    f   How do you know each triangle is isosceles?

3. PQR is an isosceles triangle with its line of symmetry passing through P(1,6) and T(5,6).

    a   Where is Q if R is the point R(4,1)?
    b   Where is R if Q is the point Q(10,5)?
    c   Where is R if Q is the point Q(4,9)?
    d   Measure the angles of this triangle.
    e   What is special about this triangle?

4. a   Measure the size of the angles of each triangle of question 2, recording your results in a table like the one below.

Triangle	Size of angle	Size of angle	Size of angle	Sum of angles
ABC	∠ABC =	∠ACB =	∠BAC =	
EFG	∠EFG =			
HIJ				
KLM				

    b   Name the equal angles in each triangle.

c   We can cut up an isosceles triangle and form the pieces as a rectangle.

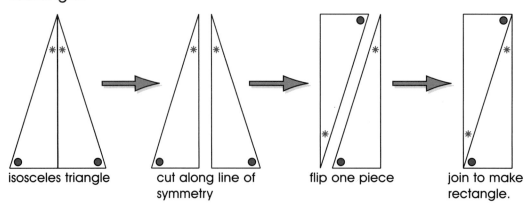

| isosceles triangle | cut along line of symmetry | flip one piece | join to make rectangle. |

How does this set of drawings help explain the last column of the table?

d   Copy and complete each sentence:
   ✤ An isosceles triangle has .... equal sides.
   ✤ The third side is called the ....
   ✤ The angles at the base are ....
   ✤ An isosceles triangle has a .... of symmetry.

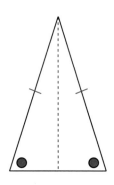

3   The Equilateral Triangle

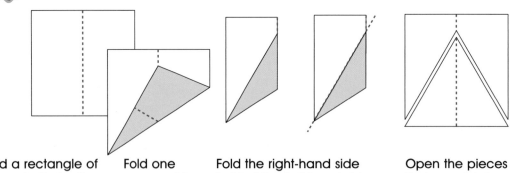

Fold a rectangle of paper to find a line of symmetry.

Fold one corner of the rectangle up to meet the the line.

Fold the right-hand side behind the left-hand side and cut along the diagonal edge of the paper.

Open the pieces out to find an odd shape and a triangle.

This could only happen if all the sides were equal and all the angles were equal.

The word *equilateral* means 'of equal sides'. An equilateral triangle has equal sides.

A

1. Five of these triangles are equilateral. Measure the sides to find the odd one out.

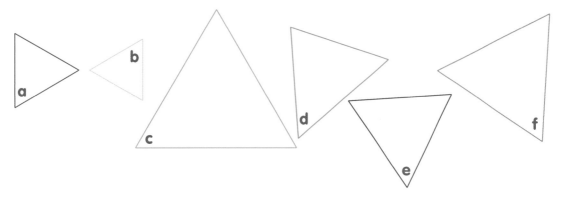

2. a How many lines of symmetry has the equilateral triangle?
    b Make an equilateral triangle by the method shown on page 106 and mark on it the lines of symmetry.
       Glue your triangle into your jotter and label it 'Equilateral'.

3. Follow the steps below to draw an accurate equilateral triangle.

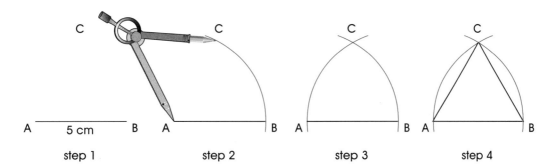

    step 1   step 2   step 3   step 4

    Step 1. Draw a 5 cm line. Call it AB.
    Step 2. Use compasses to draw an arc with a centre at A and a radius of 5 cm (AB).
    Step 3. Draw another arc of the same size with the centre at B this time.
    Step 4. Call where the arcs cross C. Draw the triangle ABC.

    Since you made sure that each length was 5 cm, then ABC is an equilateral triangle.

4. a On centimetre squared paper draw a set of coordinate axes.
    b Plot the points M(2,1), N(4,5) and P(6,1).
    c Is triangle MNP an equilateral triangle?
       Use the method above to make an equilateral triangle with one side MP. Do the arcs cross at N?

4 Rigidity

Triangles are important to engineers.

Look at the picture of this bridge.

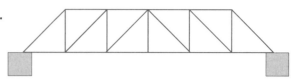

A

1. How many right-angled triangles can you see in the bridge?

2. Using geo-strips and paper fasteners form:

    a a triangle   b a square   c a rectangle   d a 5-sided figure.

3. To say a shape is rigid means it cannot change shape.
    Which of the above shapes are rigid?

4. Try to make the remaining shapes rigid by adding more geo-strip ... as
    little as you have to.
    Make sketches of your successful results and colour any triangles you have
    made.

◆ Investigate

Look through
magazines and the
Internet and gather
together pictures
that show the
importance of the
rigidity of the
triangle to the
engineer.

Unit 14 Area

1 Looking Back

1. Find the area of each shape by counting complete squares.
   Each small square is an area of 1 square centimetre (1 cm²).

   a   b   c

2. Which two shapes below have the same area?

   a   b   c   d

3. The diagram is a plan of a
   garden.
   Each square represents 1 m².
   Calculate the area of

   a the lawn   b the flowerbed.

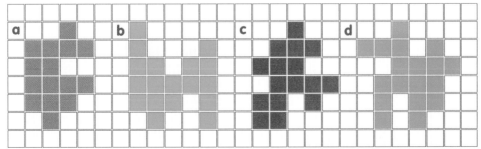

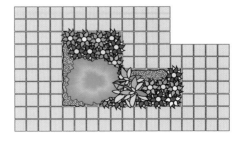

4. Find the area of each shape by counting squares and half-squares.
(Each square represents 1 cm².)

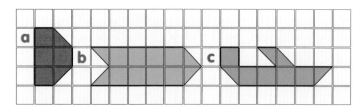

5. a Check that each shape opposite has an area
of 4 cm².
   b On centimetre squared paper draw three
more shapes with the same area.
   c Draw six different shapes, each with an area
of 8 cm².

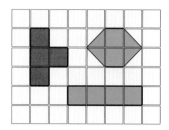

6.
square centimetre (cm²)   or   square metre (m²)

Which unit of measurement would you use to measure the area of:

a the classroom floor   b your maths jotter
c your hand   d the playground?

7. An oil tanker has leaked oil into
the sea. An oil slick has formed.

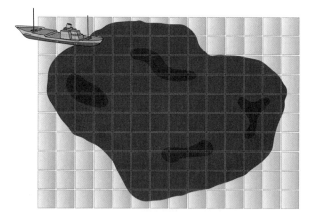

In the diagram each square
represents 1 m².

If less than half a square is
covered in oil, count it as
0 square metres.
If half a square or more is
covered in oil, count it as
1 square metre.

Calculate the area of the oil
slick.

8. On a sheet of 1 centimetre squared paper
draw an outline of your hand.

a Calculate the area of your hand.
   b Does it matter if your fingers are spread
or kept beside each other?
Explain.

2 Counting Squares the Easy Way

1. For each rectangle:

   a Write down the number of squares in each row.
   b Write down the number of rows.
   c Calculate the area. (Each square represents 1 cm².)

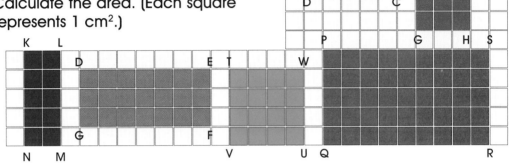

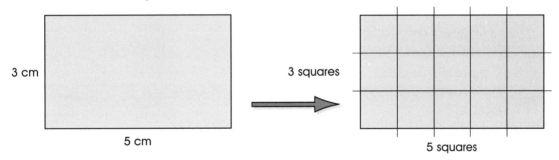

2. Imagine a square grid is placed on the rectangle. Its area is now easy to find.

3 rows of 5 squares, so the area is 3 × 5 = 15 cm².

In the same way, imagine a square centimetre grid is placed on top of each rectangle.

   i How many squares are there in each row?
   ii How many rows?
   iii Calculate the area.

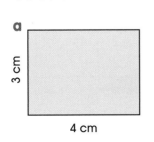

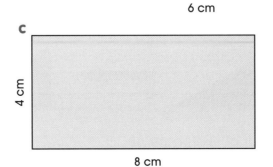

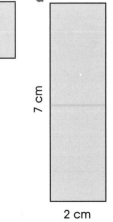

3. Find the area of each carpet.

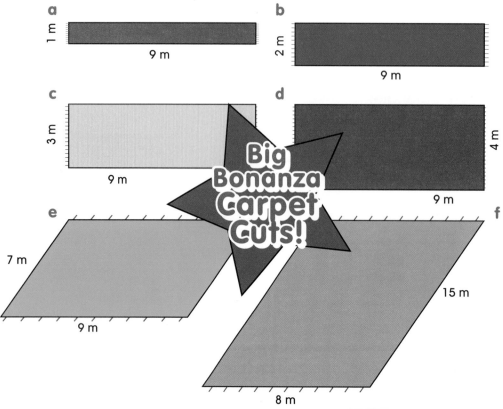

a
1 m
9 m

b
2 m
9 m

c
3 m
9 m

d
4 m
9 m

Big
Bonanza
Carpet
Cuts!

e
7 m
9 m

f
15 m
8 m

4. The Wiltons have bought an 8 metre by 6 metre rectangular carpet in the sale.

    a Calculate its area.
    b How much did the Wiltons pay for their carpet?

Grand Carpet
Sale
All carpets £9 per m²

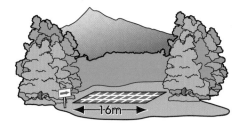

16m

5. A picnic site is square. Its length of side is 16 metres.
    The picnic site needs to be tiled with square, concrete slabs of side 1 metre.

    a How many slabs are needed?
    b What is the area of the picnic site?

3 The Area of a Right-angled Triangle

Every right-angled triangle is half of a rectangle.

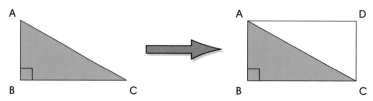

A
B   C

A   D
B   C

Triangle ABC is half of rectangle ABCD.
So the area of triangle ABC = half the area of rectangle ABCD.

A

Each square represents 1 square centimetre.

1. Count squares to help you find the area of each right-angled triangle.

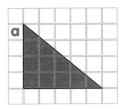 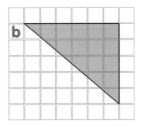 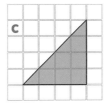 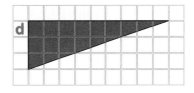

2. Find the area of each right-angled triangle by imagining a rectangle round each one.

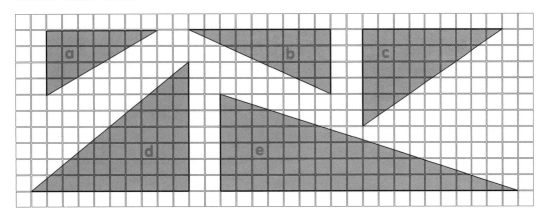

3. a Draw each of these right-angled triangles onto centimetre squared paper. Use the measurements given.
   b Find the area of each triangle.

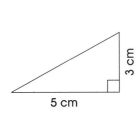 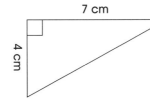 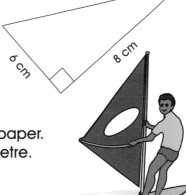

4. a Draw the sail on centimetre squared paper. Use 1 square to represent 1 square metre.
   b Find the area of the sail.

5. A ramp takes cars from the street to the car park.

   a Draw the triangular part of the ramp on centimetre squared paper. Use 1 square to represent 1 m².
   b Work out the area of this triangle.

3m

11m

1. Triangle PQR is made from two right-angled triangles.

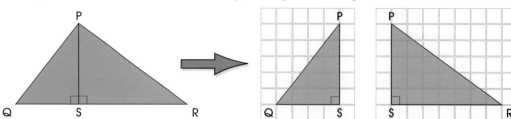

Work out the area of triangle PQR.

2. Use the same method as in question 1 to find the area of:

    a   ABC
    b   TUV

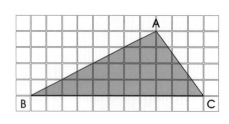
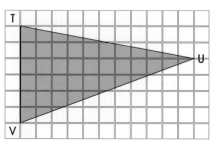

(Each square represents 1 square
centimetre.)

3. This kite has been made from four
    right-angled triangles.

    a   Find the area of each triangle.
    b   Calculate the area of the kite.

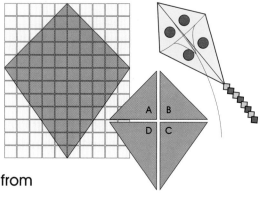

4. This parallelogram has been made from
    two right-angled triangles.

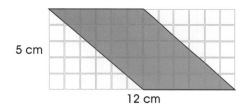

5 cm

12 cm

    a   Find the area of each triangle.
    b   Find the area of the parallelogram.

5. Logos are designed for the tail fin of an airline. The logos below have been
    designed using right-angled triangles on square centimetre grids.
    Calculate the coloured area in each logo.

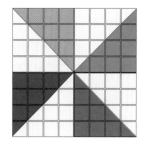
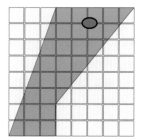
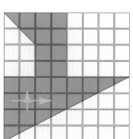

Challenge 1

A tangram is a square which has been cut up into seven pieces as shown and then rearranged to form a picture.

a Work out the area of each of the seven pieces.
b What is the area of the large square?
c What is the area of the cat?
d The man is a tangram and is thus made from all seven pieces. What is the area of the man? See if you can find out how to make the man.

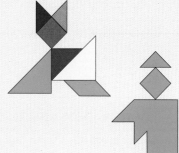

Challenge 2

a Draw this diagram on 1 cm squared paper.

AB = 12 cm, BC = 16 cm.
Angle ABC = 90°.
AD = DC. BE = EC.
Angle DEC = 90°.
DF = FC. EG = GC.
Angle FGC = 90°.

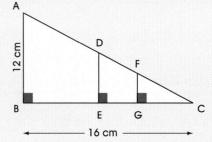

b Find the area of triangle FGC.
c Continue the pattern on your drawing to find the area of   HIC, where H is midway between F and C and I is midway between G and C. What do you notice?

4   Small Areas

1 cm² = 100 mm²

We use square millimetres for the areas of small objects.

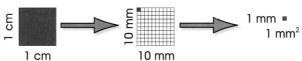

1. Which of these areas are best measured in square millimetres?

a The cover of your maths book
b Your thumbnail
c A CD case
d A postage stamp
e The wing of a house fly
f The face of a wrist watch
g The face of a clock
h The head of a drawing pin

2. Estimate these areas in square millimetres.

 a Your pinkie nail   c The surface of a one penny coin
 b A ladybird   d Your neighbour's front tooth

3. Change the following areas to square millimetres [1 cm² = 100 mm²]:

 a 1 cm²   b 7 cm²   c 12 cm²   d 15 cm²
 e 7·5 cm²   f 20 cm²   g 8·75 cm²   h 3·14 cm²

4. Change these areas to square centimetres:

 a 600 mm²   b 1400 mm²   c 10 000 mm²   d 25 000 mm²
 e 725 mm²   f 850 mm²   g 1650 mm²   h 192·5 mm²

5. Calculate the area of the stamp.

 a in square centimetres   b in square millimetres.

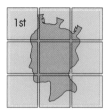

6. Estimate the area of the sticker in square millimetres.

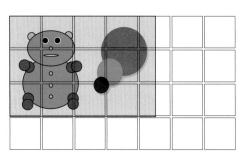

70 mm

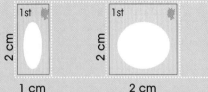

Investigate

2 cm — 1 cm
2 cm — 2 cm
2 cm — 3 cm

A postage stamp designer is trying different sizes.
The perforations form a 1 mm border all the way round the stamp.

 a When the stamp is 1 cm by 2 cm, the border has an area of 64 mm².
 b What is the area of the border when the stamp is:
    ❖ 2 cm by 2 cm   ❖ 2 cm by 3 cm?
 c What is the area of the border when the stamp is 3 cm by 5 cm?
 d Can you state a rule for finding the area of the border when the
    length and breadth are known?

Unit 15 — Whole Numbers

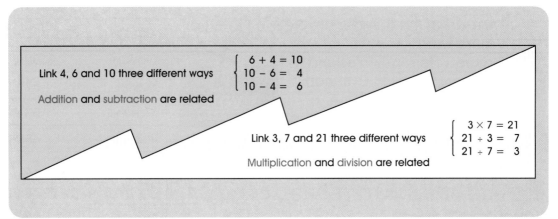

Link 4, 6 and 10 three different ways
$$\begin{cases} 6 + 4 = 10 \\ 10 - 6 = 4 \\ 10 - 4 = 6 \end{cases}$$

Addition and subtraction are related

Link 3, 7 and 21 three different ways
$$\begin{cases} 3 \times 7 = 21 \\ 21 \div 3 = 7 \\ 21 \div 7 = 3 \end{cases}$$

Multiplication and division are related

1 Looking Back

Read, write and order

1. The number of visitors to Scotland last year from some foreign countries are given in the table.

    Write in words the number of visitors from each of these countries.

Country	Number of visitors
Spain	64 075
Italy	92 406
France	67 025
Germany	240 680
United States	308 975

2. Listed below are the number of visitors last year from Scotland to some overseas countries:

Germany	fifty thousand, three hundred and twenty-five
Italy	seventy-nine thousand and eighty-five
France	one hundred and twenty thousand, six hundred and thirty
United States	one hundred and forty-eight thousand, five hundred and six

Write in figures the number of visitors to each country.

3. The number of new blood donors in Scotland each year over a six-year period are:

Year	1998	1999	2000	2001	2002	2003
Number of new donors	45 275	35 721	38 762	37 265	40 140	36 241

Put the number of new donors in order, starting with the largest.

4. The table gives the number of people in ten areas of Glasgow who can vote at an election.

Area of Glasgow	Voters
Anniesland	53 397
Baillieston	49 062
Cathcart	50 429
Govan	50 870
Kelvin	57 058
Maryhill	53 506
Pollock	48 303
Rutherglen	51 059
Shettleston	48 209
Springburn	53 427

a Put the areas in order of size starting with the smallest.
Write down the number of voters in the area if there were:

b 3 more voters in Anniesland
c 600 more voters in Cathcart
d 30 more voters in Govan
e 1000 more voters in Baillieston
f 1000 less voters in Govan
g 10 less voters in Pollock
h 100 less voters in Rutherglen.

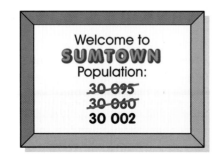

Welcome to
SUMTOWN
Population:
~~30 095~~
~~30 060~~
30 002

5. The population of Sumtown at the end of 2000 was 30 002.
During 2001 it fell by 10.
In 2002 it rose by 100.
The following year it rose by 10.
In 2004 it fell by 200.

Write down the population of Sumtown at the end of:

a 2001   b 2002   c 2003   d 2004.

Calculations

1. Add:

a	342 $+\ 427$	b	419 $+\ 453$	c	186 $+\ 315$	d	705 $+\ 648$
e	3245 $+\ 5734$	f	1648 $+\ 7237$	g	5264 $+\ 3683$	h	4748 $+\ 2391$

i 3612 + 1785 + 2648   j 5312 + 6794 + 8056

2. Subtract:

a	847 $-\ 315$	b	764 $-\ 129$	c	819 $-\ 576$	d	650 $-\ 432$	e	904 $-\ 371$
f	600 $-\ 487$	g	7234 $-\ 4006$	h	9647 $-\ 3481$	i	6458 $-\ 2749$	j	3740 $-\ 267$

k 7518 $-\ 945$ l 7146 + 2418 − 4395   m 9000 − 3256 + 6308

3. Work out:

a   234
   ×   5

b   586
   ×   7

c   709
   ×   6

d   645
   ×   9

e   4325
   ×   6

f   7168
   ×   5

g   9416
   ×   8

h   3574
   ×   9

4. Do the following divisions:

a   185 ÷ 5   b   581 ÷ 7   c   837 ÷ 9   d   608 ÷ 8
e   5663 ÷ 7   f   4428 ÷ 6   g   5157 ÷ 9   h   6905 ÷ 5

5. Find the remainder:

a   389 ÷ 7   b   762 ÷ 9   c   8617 ÷ 6   d   6453 ÷ 8

6. Calculate the number that comes out of each of these function machines:

a

IN   OUT

b

IN   OUT

Rounding

1. Round these numbers to the nearest 10:

a 78   b 93   c 65   d 114   e 127   f 884
g 306   h 215   i 2631   j 4819   k 7026   l 9495

2. Round these to the nearest 100:

a 82   b 314   c 654   d 250   e 980   f 1271
g 2350   h 8089   i 56 490 j 63 173   k 82 748   l 31 150

3. Round these to the nearest 1000:

a 703   b 4613   c 8234   d 9605   e 3500   f 9378
g 18 309 h 78 269 i 80 711 j 66 666   k 75 500   l 99 950

4. Round these sums of money to the nearest £:

a £2·72   b £9·38   c £34·62   d £111·50

5. Round the measurements to the nearest metre:

a 4 m 72 cm   b 9 m 46 cm   c 78 m 50 cm   d 6 m 8 cm

6. Round to the nearest kilogram:

a | 4 kg 780 g | b | 58 kg 475 g | c | 42 kg 500 g | d | 12 kg 89 g

7. Round to the nearest hour:

   a 6 hours 34 minutes   b 12 hours 48 minutes   c 10 hours 30 minutes

8. Estimate the answer to each calculation by first rounding each number to the nearest 100:

   a 734 + 482 + 293   b 3742 + 4941 – 6084   c 9382 – 4709 – 3390

2 Making Use of Numbers

1. Sal buys a computer for £985 and a printer for £128.
   What is the total cost?

Lochgreen
Population:
9476

2. a 5348 males live in Lochgreen.
      How many females live in Lochgreen?
   b 1685 people are left-handed.
      How many are not left-handed?
   c 2869 teenagers live in Lochgreen.
      How many residents are not teenagers?

3. A charity relay is being run over the 603 miles from Land's End to John o'Groats.
   Each runner runs 9 miles.
   How many runners are needed?

John O'Groats

Land's End

4. Each morning a milkman delivers 647 bottles of milk and 186 tubs of cream.

   a How many bottles of milk are delivered each week?
   b How many tubs of cream?
   c How many more bottles of milk are delivered each week than tubs of cream?

5. Seven people deliver a total of 7882 leaflets.
   They all deliver the same number each.
   How many leaflets does each person deliver?

6. Melanie drives from Madrid to Paris and then to Copenhagen.

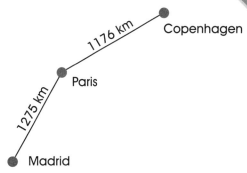

   a How far does she drive in total?
   b How much further is the drive to Paris than the drive to Copenhagen?

7. 8365 people at a rock concert each paid £8 for a ticket.
   How much money was made from the sale of tickets?

 B

1. There are eight jars of honey in a case.

   a How many cases can be made with 5000 jars?
   b How many jars are needed to fill 1725 cases?

2. A machine can make eight flower pots every minute.
   How many flower pots can it make in 12 hours?

3. The table gives information about the runners in a London marathon.
   Use the table to help you answer these questions:

   a How many female runners were there?
   b How many male runners did not finish?
   c How many female runners did not finish?
   d How many runners took between 3 and 4 hours?
   e All runners had to pay an entry fee of £7. How much money was collected from entry fees?
   f Each runner was given a one-third litre bottle of water.
     How many litres of water were given in total to the runners?

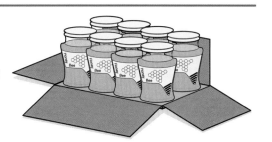

	Number of runners
All runners	9318
Male runners	4762
Male finishers	3465
Female finishers	3709
Time:	
Less than 3 hours	948
More than 4 hours	2475

4.

Price £7650   Price £9225   Price £5199

Mileage 24 540   Mileage 8360   Mileage 37 210

a What is the total price of the three cars?
b What is the difference in price between the dearest and the cheapest car?
c What is the difference between the highest and the lowest mileage?
d How many more miles before the dearest car has travelled 10 000 miles?

Challenge

1. Find the smallest whole number that can be divided evenly by 2, 3, 4, 5, 6, 7, 8 and 9.

2. The charges for the funicular railway up the Cairngorms mountains are:

2 adults and up to 3 children	£22
1 adult and up to 2 children	£16
1 adult	£7.50
1 child	£5
Senior citizen/Student	£6

a A party of 7 adults and 12 children wish to use the railway.
What is the cheapest way for them to travel?
b One of the adults is a senior citizen.
What is now the cheapest way for them to travel?

---

3   **Counting on the Calculator**

When using a calculator, always estimate, calculate and check your answers.

Example   Calculate 4843 + 2367.

     Estimate   Round the numbers to get a rough answer:
                   5000 + 2000 = 7000.
     Calculate   Use your calculator: 4834 + 2367 = 7201.
     Check   Compare the calculator answer with the estimate:
                   Yes, 7201 agrees roughly with 7000.

A

1. Copy and complete the table.

	Problem	Estimate	Calculate	Check
a	589 + 213	600 + 200 = 800	802	802 is close to 800
b	884 − 675	900 − 700 =		
c	6043 × 11	6000 × 10 =		
d	9438 ÷ 13	9000 ÷ 10 =		
e	909 + 488			
f	4314 − 827			
g	121 × 98			
h	9603 ÷ 99			

2. Calculate the following. (Round each number to the nearest thousand where appropriate.)

    a 6587 + 3904 + 6284   b 7214 − 1856 + 8372   c 486 × 265 ÷ 81

3. Simone earns £627 each week.
   How much does she earn in a year?

Check your answer to make sure it is sensible

4. Ali earns £8112 a year at the supermarket.
   How much does he earn each: a week   b month?

5. 7465 people at a rock concert each paid £29 for their ticket.
   How much money was made from the sale of the tickets?

6. The grids show the last two gas meter readings at the Watsons' house.

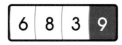 

   a How many units of gas have been used between readings?
   b Each unit of gas costs 17 pence.
      How much will the Watsons have to pay for the gas used?

B

In each of the following check your answer to make sure it is sensible.

1. The number of votes given to each candidate at an election is shown in the table.

Candidate	Number of votes
B. Cool	3692
T. Time	5481
L. Ping	8362
M. Tee	783
C. Ewe	2165

    a   Who won the election?
    b   How many more votes did the winner get than the candidate who came second?
    c   What was the difference in the number of votes between the winner and the person who was last?
    d   How many people voted at the election?

2. A sports store bought 35 pairs of trainers.

    a   What was the total cost of the trainers?
    b   The store sold the trainers at £39 a pair. Calculate the profit they made.

3. The table shows the number of loaves and the number of rolls sold last week by the baker.

Item	Number sold	Price
Brown loaf	897	72p
White loaf	5765	67p
Rolls (pack of 6)	3802	59p
Rolls (pack of 4)	2718	42p

    a   What was the total number of loaves sold?
    b   How many packs of rolls were sold?
    How much money was made from the sale of:
    c   loaves   d   rolls?

4. Polly's Pizza Parlour employs six people. Their monthly wages are:

    £2094, £1645, £1189, £1026, £786, £786

    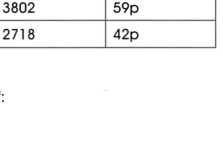
    Polly's Pizza Parlour

    a   Calculate the total monthly wage bill.
    b   What is the annual wage bill?
    c   What is the annual wage of the lowest paid worker?
    d   What is the annual wage of the highest paid worker?

Equations

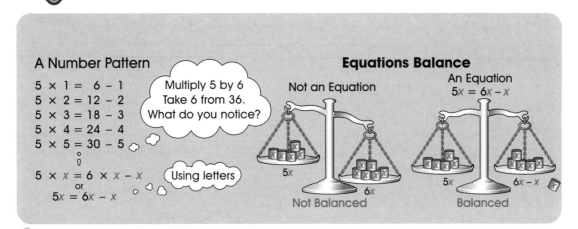

A Number Pattern

$5 \times 1 = 6 - 1$
$5 \times 2 = 12 - 2$
$5 \times 3 = 18 - 3$
$5 \times 4 = 24 - 4$
$5 \times 5 = 30 - 5$

$5 \times x = 6 \times x - x$
or
$5x = 6x - x$

Multiply 5 by 6
Take 6 from 36.
What do you notice?

Using letters

Equations Balance

Not an Equation

An Equation
$5x = 6x - x$

$5x$

$6x$

Not Balanced

$5x$

$6x - x$

Balanced

1 Looking Back

1. What number is covered?

   a $3 + \bigcirc = 7$ b $12 - \bigcirc = 5$ c $3 \times \bigcirc = 15$ d $25 \div \bigcirc = 5$

2. Find the value of each letter, writing your answer like this: $x = 8$

   a
   $\boxed{x}$ $\boxed{17}$ → Total 19
   $\boxed{y}$ $\boxed{z}$ → Total 13
   ↓   ↓
   Total 10   Total w

   b
   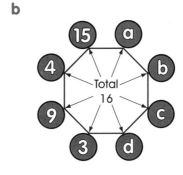
   15 a
   4   b
   Total 16
   9   c
   3 d

3. Find the value of each letter:

   a

   Total 19

   b
   7 × x
   Total 17

   c
   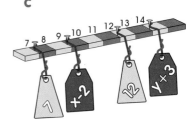

4.

2	7	6
9	5	1
4	3	8

When $n = 6$ these two magic squares are identical:

Complete the missing expressions in the square on the right.

	$n+1$	
		$n-5$
$n-2$		

2 Equations and Solutions

The EQUATION describing this picture is:

$x + 7 = 13$

To solve the equation:

$\square + 7 = 13$

6 is covered

The SOLUTION of this equation is:

$x = 6$

The scales are balanced.
All the weights are kg.

So the mystery weight is 6 kg.

1. For each picture:

   i   Write the equation for each set of scales.

   ii Find the solution of the equation.

   iii Say what the solution means (all weights are in kg).

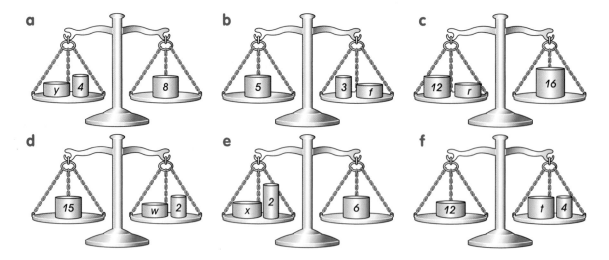

2. Solve these equations. Give the solutions like this: $y = 7$

a $x + 3 = 8$	**b** $4 + y = 6$	**c** $12 = a + 5$	**d** $13 = 5 + f$
e $x - 5 = 2$	**f** $6 = w - 3$	**g** $r + 8 = 17$	**h** $z - 6 = 7$
i $n + 2 = 11$	**j** $w - 6 = 14$	**k** $x - 6 = 0$	**l** $y - 5 = 8$
m $u + 4 = 10$	**n** $m + 5 = 16$	**o** $d + 2 = 21$	**p** $c - 6 = 2$

3. For the number machine

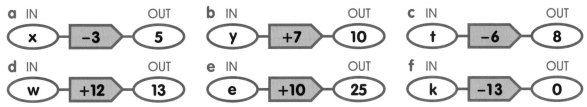

IN   OUT

x — $+7$ — 13

we can write the equation $x + 7 = 13$.

Write equations for each of the following machines, then solve them.

a IN — OUT
x — -3 — 5

b IN — OUT
y — $+7$ — 10

c IN — OUT
t — -6 — 8

d IN — OUT
w — $+12$ — 13

e IN — OUT
e — $+10$ — 25

f IN — OUT
k — -13 — 0

Example 1

There was 200 ml of paint.
x ml spilled.
There is now 150 ml left.

How much was spilled?

The EQUATION describing this situation is:

$$200 - x = 150$$
$$200 - \text{☐} = 150$$
so $x = 50$

50 ml of paint was spilled.

Example 2

There was x ml of paint.
50 ml spilled.
There is now 150 ml left.

How much paint was there?

The EQUATION describing this situation is:

$$x - 50 = 150$$
$$\text{☐} - 50 = 150$$
so $x = 50$

There was 200 ml of paint.

B

1. Write an equation suggested by each picture, solve it and say what the solution means.

a There was 300 ml in the flask.
y ml spilled.
There is now 250 ml left.

How much has spilled?

b There was w ml in the flask.
25 ml spilled.
There is now 375 ml left.

How much was in the flask to start with?

c £x is removed from the bag leaving £19.

£26

How much was removed?

d The Memo Pad has m pages.
Graeme used 12 pages and there are 26 left.

NOTE BOOK

How many pages were in the pad to begin with?

e A ladder has 30 rungs.
r rungs are broken leaving 23 safe rungs.

How many were broken?

f I remove £6 from the bag leaving £17.

£x

How much was in the bag to start with?

Challenge

Study each picture. One or two equations should jump to mind. Complete the grid.

Clues Across

1

total 9

4 x litres spilled leaving only 5 litres

5 I ate x chocolates!

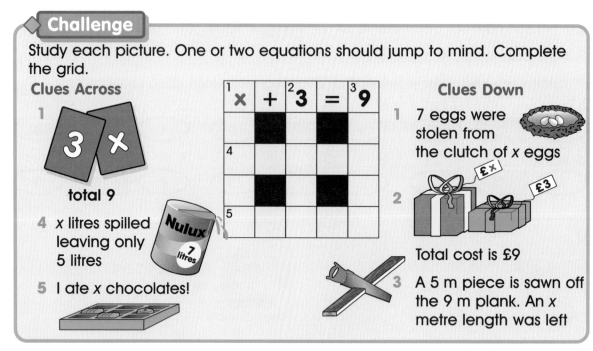

Clues Down

1 7 eggs were stolen from the clutch of x eggs

2 Total cost is £9

3 A 5 m piece is sawn off the 9 m plank. An x metre length was left

---

3 The Equations are Multiplying

The **EQUATION** describing this situation is:

$$5x = 20$$

The **SOLUTION** of this equation is:

$$x = 4$$

To solve the equation:

$$5 \times \bigcirc = 20$$

4 is covered

So each weight on the left weighs 4 kg.

A

1. For each picture:

   i write the equation that describes the situation

   ii find the solution of the equation

   iii say what the solution means (all weights are in kg)

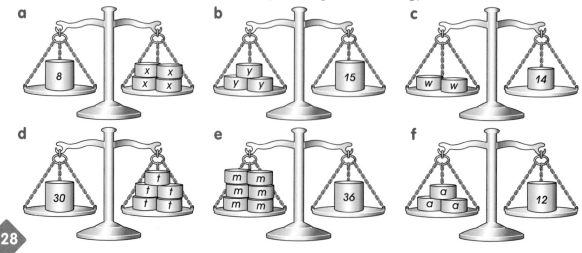

2. Solve these equations. Give the solutions like this: $x = 4$.

a $7x = 56$	b $30 = 3y$	c $2h = 10$	d $4x = 8$	e $6 = 2e$
f $5g = 30$	g $4a = 20$	h $45 = 5n$	i $72 = 9b$	j $7m = 21$
k $8z = 40$	l $6t = 42$	m $9c = 54$	n $70 = 10w$	o $8k = 80$

3. For each number machine write an equation and solve it to find the **IN** number.

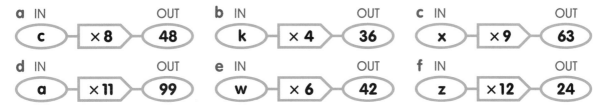

a IN   OUT   c ─ ×8 ─ 48

b IN   OUT   k ─ ×4 ─ 36

c IN   OUT   x ─ ×9 ─ 63

d IN   OUT   a ─ ×11 ─ 99

e IN   OUT   w ─ ×6 ─ 42

f IN   OUT   z ─ ×12 ─ 24

Challenge

Clues Across

1   $x + 8 = 32$
3   $2x = 84$
5   $119 = 7x$
6   $10x = 130$
7   $x - 10 = 1$
9   $x + 17 = 100$
11   $5x = 100$
12   $130 = 2x$
13   $15 + x = 40$
15   $6x = 90$
17   $92 = 4x$
19   $45 - x = 15$
20   $5x = 80$
21   $23 = x + 9$

Clues Down

1   $108 = 4x$
2   $53 - x = 12$
3   $34 = x - 9$
4   $5x = 105$
5   $11 = x - 7$
8   $31 = 21 + x$
10   $3x = 105$
11   $176 = 8x$
12   $46 = x - 15$
14   $22 = 72 - x$
16   $102 = 2x$
17   $41 - x = 15$
18   $7x = 217$
19   $16 + x = 50$

Example

The scales are balanced.
All the weights are kg.

For this situation the equation is:

$3x + 9 = 30$

$3x = 21$

$x = 7$

Step 1 in solving is:
$\bigcirc + 9 = 30$
21 is covered

Step 2 in solving is:
$3 \times \bigcirc = 21$
7 is covered

B

1. For each picture:
   i   write the equation that describes the situation
   ii find the solution of the equation
   iii say what the solution means (all weights are in kg)

   In each case check that your solution balances the scales!

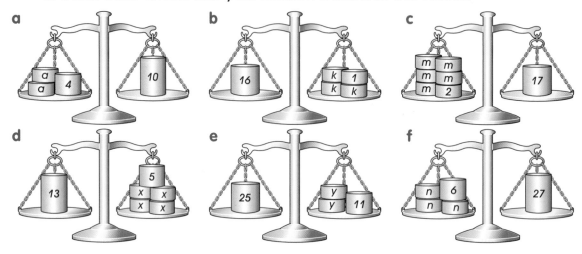

2. For each number machine, write an equation and solve it to find the **IN** number. Check in each case that your **IN** number does give the **OUT** number.

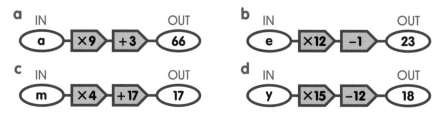

3. Solve these equations. (Remember to check your solution in each case by putting the value back into the equation.) Does it balance?

   a $8a + 2 = 34$ b $40 = 7y + 5$ c $8h - 1 = 79$
   d $9z + 10 = 91$ e $7x - 3 = 11$ f $7 = 5g - 3$
   g $11q + 4 = 15$ h $6f - 5 = 13$ i $4d + 7 = 19$
   j $56 = 9m + 11$ k $9 = 2b + 9$

4. a Iain buys three hooded sweatshirts. They cost £x each.
      Write an expression for the total cost of the sweatshirts.
   b He also bought a belt for £6.
      What has he spent in total?
   c If he spent £57 in total, write an equation and solve it to find the cost of one sweatshirt.

5. a Kathryn buys four CDs.
If they cost £y each write an expression
for their total cost.

b She also bought a shoulder bag for £12.
Write an expression for her total spending
so far.

c Her total spending was in fact £40.
Make an equation and solve it to find the cost of one CD.

6. a Alasdair spent £8 on a video and then
bought three batteries.
Write an expression for the total cost if
each battery cost £x.

b He spent £17.
Make an equation and solve it to find the cost of one battery.

7. a Katrina bought eight cakes and a £5 bread knife.
Write an expression for the total cost.

b If she spent £21 make an equation and solve it to find the cost of a
cake.

Challenge

The Shapes Puzzle

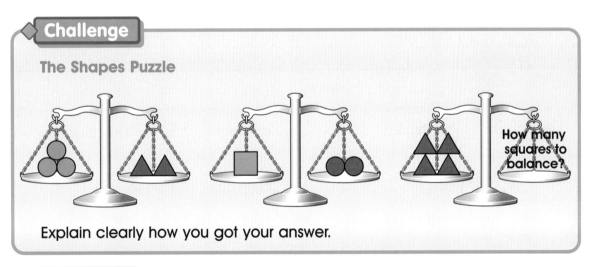

How many
squares to
balance?

Explain clearly how you got your answer.

Challenge

The Crowded Balance Puzzle

What does ☐ weigh?

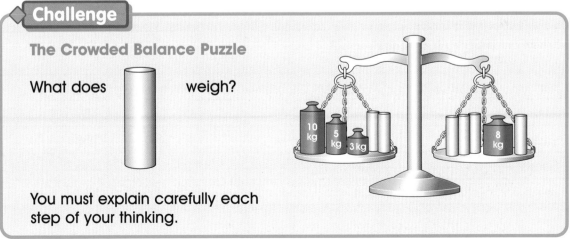

You must explain carefully each
step of your thinking.

Information Handling

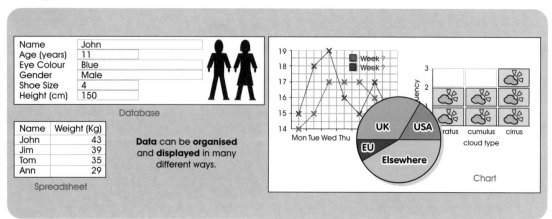

Name	John
Age (years)	11
Eye Colour	Blue
Gender	Male
Shoe Size	4
Height (cm)	150

Database

Name	Weight (Kg)
John	43
Jim	39
Tom	35
Ann	29

Spreadsheet

Data can be **organised** and **displayed** in many different ways.

Chart

1 Looking Back

Here are four **records** of a **database**. Each record holds six categories of information called **fields**.

Name	Craig
Age (years)	12
Eye colour	Brown
Gender	M
Shoe size	5
Height (cm)	158

Name	Alex
Age (years)	12
Eye colour	Brown
Gender	M
Shoe size	6
Height (cm)	159

Name	Sarah
Age (years)	12
Eye colour	Blue
Gender	F
Shoe size	5
Height (cm)	156

Name	Leigh
Age (years)	11
Eye colour	Blue
Gender	F
Shoe size	4
Height (cm)	151

A different **layout** could be used to save having to list the names of the fields each time.

Each record now occupies a **row** and each field, a **column**.

In this layout it is easy to **sort** the data by different fields. Here they have been sorted by height, tallest first.

Name	Age (yrs)	Eye colour	Gender	Shoe size	Height (cm)
Alex	12	Brown	M	6	159
Craig	12	Brown	M	5	158
Sarah	12	Blue	F	5	156
Leigh	11	Blue	F	4	151

1. What are the fields making up the database?

2. How may records are there for boys?

3. **a** What height is Craig? **b** What colour are Sarah's eyes?
   c Who has size 4 feet? **d** Who is smaller than 155 cm?

4. **a** Copy and complete this table using the information from field 'Eye Colour'.
   b Draw a bar graph to display this data.
   c What are the most common eye colours?

Eye Colour	Frequency
Blue	
Green	
Hazel	
Brown	

5. **a** Copy and complete this table using the information from the database about height.
   b Copy the diagram and complete a frequency polygon to display this data.
   c What height is the tallest pupil?
   d Which two of the height intervals have the same frequency?

Height (cm)	Frequency
140–143	
144–147	
148–151	
152–155	
156–159	
160–163	

Heights

Frequency

3
2
1
0
140 144 148 152 156 160
Height (cm)

6. A class was given a test of 100 questions.
   The number of correct answers each pupil gave is listed below.

65	78	63	88	92	51	64
67	83	69	52	90	45	74
73	67	58	63	81	71	65
73	71	68	15	38	79	96

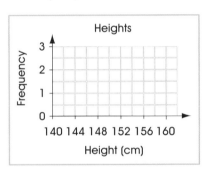

$\dfrac{96}{100}$ Very well done

a Copy and complete this table:
b Use a suitable graph to display this data.
c What was the difference between the highest and lowest marks?
d If the pass mark was 60 out of 100, how many pupils passed the test?

Mark	Tally	Total
1–20		
21–40		
41–60		
61–80		
81–100		

2 Pie Charts – Display the Data

Mike and Maureen had been plane spotting at the airport.
One sixth ($\frac{1}{6}$) of the flights out were to the USA.
One third ($\frac{1}{3}$) were domestic flights.
One twelfth ($\frac{1}{12}$) went to the European Union.
The rest went elsewhere.

This sort of data is best shown by means of a pie chart.

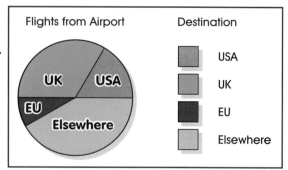

1. The Primary 6 Enterprise Group held a School Fête and raised lots of money for charity.
   They decided to split the money, giving $\frac{1}{2}$ to a local guide dog organisation, $\frac{1}{4}$ to a children's hospital and the rest to a pet sanctuary.

   They wish to use a pie chart to illustrate the share-out.

   a Draw a circle and a radius.
   b Calculate $\frac{1}{2}$ of 360° and then draw a sector to represent the money that went to the guide dog association.
   c Calculate $\frac{1}{4}$ of 360° and then draw a sector to represent the money that went to the children's hospital.
   d Show on your chart the sector representing the money that went to the pet sanctuary.
   e Add a title and a key to make it clear what your chart is all about.

2. A vote is taken in Primary 7 to decide where to go on the school outing. One third voted for the Science Centre; two thirds voted for the Outdoor Centre.

   a Draw a circle and a radius.
   b Calculate $\frac{1}{3}$ of 360°. Draw a sector to represent the pupils who voted for the Science Centre.
   c Label the sector that represents those who wished to go to the Outdoor Centre.
   d Add a title and a key.

3. A survey was done of the weeds in the playing fields.
   $\frac{1}{5}$ of the weeds were buttercups, $\frac{1}{10}$ of them were dandelions, $\frac{3}{8}$ were daisies and the rest were clover.

   Calculate

   a $\frac{1}{5}$ of 360°   b $\frac{1}{10}$ of 360°   c $\frac{3}{8}$ of 360° (hint: find $\frac{1}{8}$ first)
   d Draw a pie chart to show the findings of the survey.

4. A survey was carried out at Pobbleburn Primary on the way pupils get to school.
It was found that 0·4 of the children walk; that 0·3 are driven; that 0·2 cycle and the rest take the bus.

Calculate:
a 0·4 of 360°
b 0·3 of 360°
c 0·2 of 360°
d Draw a pie chart to show the findings of the survey.

5. At the Transport Museum they asked the visitors which section they preferred.
'The Steam section', said 0·15 of the visitors; 'The Trams', said 0·25; and 'The Automobiles' said 0·45.
All the other visitors picked something else. (Call it 'Other'.)

Draw a pie chart to illustrate these figures.

3 Pie Charts – Fractions of a Whole

How do you like your coffee?

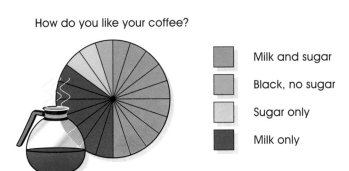

Milk and sugar

Black, no sugar

Sugar only

Milk only

From this chart we see that the circle has been broken into 20 equal parts.

The 'Sugar Only' category occupies 2 parts.

Thus 2 out of 20 take sugar only.

Written as a fraction this is $\frac{2}{20} = \frac{1}{10}$

A

1. 10 people were asked their opinion on a new movie.
The results are shown on the pie chart.

What fraction of the people thought the film was:

a Fair   b Poor
c Good   d Very Good?

Movie Reviews

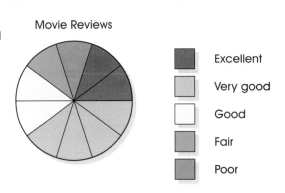

Excellent

Very good

Good

Fair

Poor

2. This pie chart shows the favourite fruits of 20 pupils.

What fraction of the pupils prefer:

a Apples   **b** Oranges
c Bananas   **d** Pears
e Grapes   **f** Peaches?
g Which two fruits are least popular?

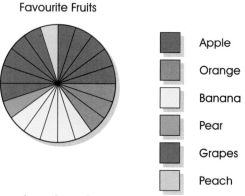

Favourite Fruits

- Apple
- Orange
- Banana
- Pear
- Grapes
- Peach

3. Tom counts the number of sweets of each colour in a bag of jelly beans.

A full bag of beans contains 60 sweets.

When he counted the sweets in the bag he found 20 red, 30 orange and 10 green.

20 out of 60 are red ... $\frac{20}{60}$ are red ... $\frac{20}{60}$ of 360 = 120 ... 120° will represent the red sweets.

In a similar way calculate the angle which will represent:
a the orange sweets   **b** the green sweets.
c Draw a pie chart to show the mix of colours in the bag.

4   Line Graphs

Here is a table of bicycle sales at a shop over a year. The figures were recorded at the end of each month.

Month	J	F	M	A	M	J	J	A	S	O	N	D
Sales	15	22	30	30	36	44	46	40	48	55	76	97

Figures like this are best shown in a line graph.

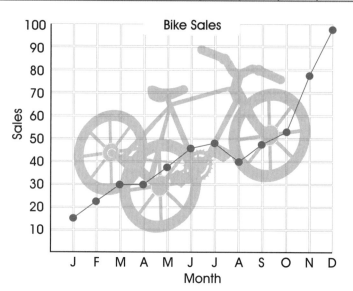

Bike Sales

1. A small ferry boat runs between the village of Lamlash on the Isle of Arran and the Holy Isle. The number of passengers is recorded at the end of each month.
   This line graph shows these monthly figures.

   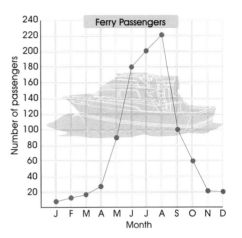

   a During which month was the ferryman:
      ❖ busiest?   ❖ quietest?
   b How many people travelled to the Holy Isle during the month of June?
   c During which month did exactly 60 passengers travel?
   d In how many months did more than 70 passengers cross?
   e Describe the **trend** shown by this graph.
      This type of trend is often called a *seasonal* trend.
      What do you think that means?

2. Jane's mum gave birth to her little baby brother Nathan. He was a tiny baby, only weighing 2.7 kg at birth. During the first three months of his life Nathan was weighed every two weeks. The results are shown below:

Age (weeks)	0	2	4	6	8	10	12
Weight (kg)	2.7	2.8	3.0	3.3	3.8	4.4	4.9

   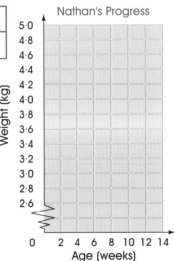

   a Copy and complete the line graph to display Nathan's progress.
   b How much weight did baby Nathan put on between birth and 12 weeks?
   c When was Nathan putting on weight most quickly?
   d Describe the **trend** shown by this graph.
   e What is the purpose of the zig-zag on the 'Weight' axis?
   f Could the graph be used to estimate Nathan's weight in week 9?

3. An ice cream man records the number of sales he makes at each of his stops.

Stop	1	2	3	4	5	6	7
Sales	3	5	6	7	4	2	6

a Make a line graph to show the ice cream sales.
b Is there an overall trend in the graph?
c How many sales did he make at stop 3?
d How many sales did he make at stop 4?
e How many sales did he make as he travelled between stops 3 and 4? Could you have read this from the graph?
f Give one main difference between the type of data in question 2 and the type of data in question 3.

5 Handling Data on a Computer

Here is part of a **spreadsheet**.
A spreadsheet is a computer program that handles and displays data.

It looks like a table made up of **rows** (1, 2, 3, etc) and **columns** (A, B, C, etc) of **cells**.

	A	B	C
1	Day	Tickets Sold	Money Raised
2	Monday	10	£25
3	Tuesday	8	
4	Wednesday	15	
5	Thursday	6	
6	Friday	20	
7	Total		

Each cell is named after the row and column in which it is found. Cell B5 has been highlighted.

A

1. Look at the ticket sales spreadsheet above.

a In which cell is the word **Wednesday**?
b In which cell is the number **10**?
c What is in cell **A7**?
d What is in cell **B5**?
e Copy the spreadsheet and complete the cell **B7** – total tickets sold.
f Use the information given for Monday's sales to calculate the cost of one ticket.
g Calculate the money raised each day – cells **C3**, **C4**, **C5**, **C6**.
h Calculate the total money raised – cell **C7**.

2. A database is similar to a spreadsheet but is better for sorting, grouping and keeping records.
   This database records a week's weather.

Day	Noon Temp °C	Cloud type	Cloud cover	Rain (mm)	Wind speed	Wind direction
Monday	14	stratus	$\frac{7}{8}$ of sky	20	strong	W
Tuesday	15	cumulus	$\frac{6}{8}$	10	strong	NW
Wednesday	17	cirrus	$\frac{4}{8}$	0	moderate	SW
Thursday	17	cirrus	$\frac{4}{8}$	0	light	SW
Friday	17	cirrus	$\frac{4}{8}$	0	light	SW
Saturday	16	cumulus	$\frac{4}{8}$	0	light	NW
Sunday	14	stratus	$\frac{4}{8}$	18	light	NW

   a How many fields make up this database?
   b On how many days are **cirrus** clouds recorded?
   c From which of the eight main compass points did the wind *not* blow during the week?
   d Which days had a midday temperature of less than 16°C?
   e Which days had the heaviest cloud cover?
   f List the dry days.
   g Describe the wind speed over the week.
   h Sort the days out in order of noon temperature, warmest first.

3. Spreadsheets can be used to make charts. Here a spreadsheet has been used to make a pie chart of windspeed records over a month.

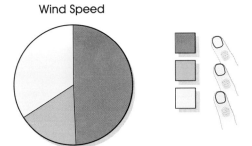

Wind Speed

Number of Days

	A	B
1	Wind speed	Number of days
2	strong	15
3	moderate	5
4	light	10

Someone is hiding the key.

   a Which colour goes with which wind speed?
   b For what fraction of the month was the wind:
      i strong   ii moderate   iii light?

4. Here is a line graph made by a spreadsheet.
   Again someone is hiding some of the data.

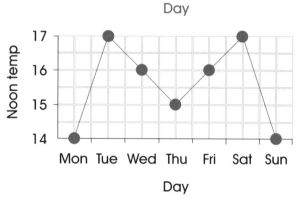

	A	B
1	Day	Noon Temp °C
2	Mon	14
3	Tue	
4	Wed	
5	Thu	
6	Fri	
7	Sat	
8	Sun	

a Copy and complete the table.
b What was the highest noon temperature in the week?
c What do you notice about the noon temperature scale?

5. Here two weeks are being compared.

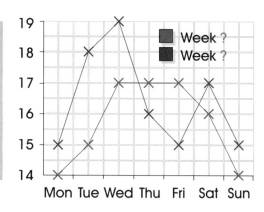

	A	B	C
1	Day	week 1 Temp	week 2 Temp
2	Mon	14	15
3	Tue	15	
4	Wed	17	
5	Thu	17	
6	Fri	17	
7	Sat	16	
8	Sun	14	

a What colour goes with each week?
b Complete the figures for week 2 in the table.
c For how many days was week 1 better than week 2?
d Which is the warmer week?

6. The pictogram created by the spreadsheet shows cloud type over the
   week.

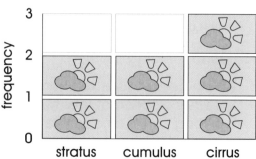

	A	B
1	Cloud type	frequency
2	stratus	
3	cumulus	
4	cirrus	

a Copy and complete the frequency table.
b What does one 'picture' represent?

Unit 18 Decimals

Speech bubble: In the late 1960's, Texas Instruments invented the world's first electronic hand-held calculator prototype

Speech bubble: It was called the Cal-Tech. It could add, subtract, multiply and divide. The answers were printed on paper tape

1 Looking Back

1. Find the answers to these additions and subtractions:

   a 15·9
      + 16·4

   b 33·25
      + 9·16

   c 14·3
      − 3·7

   d 30·1
      − 18·3

   e 28·76
      − 19·47

2. Calculate:

   a 23·74 − 5·57

   b 34·76 + 9·18

   c 42·16 − 11·85

3. Justin and Scott went camping in the Highlands for the weekend. Justin's backpack weighed 14·7 kg. Scott's backpack weighed 3·6 kg more. What was the weight of Scott's backpack?

4. The temperature in Dumfries rose from 9·7°C in the morning to 18·2°C in the afternoon. Calculate the rise in temperature that day.

5. Anne used her birthday money to buy a T-shirt for £14·75 and a Chart Hits CD for £16·99.

   a How much money did she spend?
   b How much change did she get from £50? *(Hint: Write £50 as £50·00.)*

6. Find the difference in the height of these two trees.

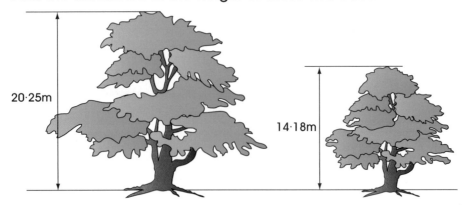

20·25m

14·18m

7. Round the following to the nearest whole number:

    a 2·6   **b** 41·5   **c** 399·7   **d** 0·9   **e** 19·99   **f** 48·55

8. Round these numbers to: **i** the nearest 10   **ii** the nearest 100.

    a 791   **b** 3726   **c** 125·6 km   **d** 234·5 kg   **e** £365·45

9. Round these numbers to the nearest whole number and **estimate** the answer to the calculation.

    a 12·5 + 3·2   **b** 14·3 – 3·8   **c** 17·3 – 9·5   **d** 13·6 + 15·7
    e 18·65 + 10·12 **f** 19·34 – 6·6   **g** 28·67 – 19·97

10. Four savings boxes have different amounts of money inside.
    Which two or three boxes together:

    a have **about** £17?
    b have **about** £20?
    c have **about** £30?

£ 12·82

£ 9·37

£ 8·49

£ 11·50

11. Do these multiplications and divisions:

    a 13·5   **b** 15·23   **c** 23·47   **d**
      × 5   × 6   × 4   4) 52·4

    e 7) 256·2   **f** 5) 61·2   **g** 5) 61·25   **h** 9) 86·58

12. Calculate:

    a 136·6 × 3   **b** 15·66 ÷ 6   **c** 10·35 ÷ 5   **d** 27·48 × 4   **e** 13·18 × 6

13. Six cartons of fresh orange juice cost £11·34.
    What is the price of one carton?

14. Sanjay changes the water in his pet fish's bowl three times a week.

   a If he uses 8·7 litres of water each time, how much water does he use in a week?

   b Round your answer to the nearest litre.

15. Hazel travels into work by bus, six days a week.

   a If she spends £2·45 on fares each day, how much does she spend in a week?

   b If she travels 27·84 km a week, what distance does she travel each day?

2 Which Operation?

A

1. Lemonade is sold on special offer in 4·2 litre bottles, $\frac{1}{3}$ of which is free.

   a What is $\frac{1}{3}$ of 4·2?

   b What size of bottle is the lemonade usually sold in?

2. Tiffany travels on the bus every day for seven days.

Bus Ticket

Weekly Ticket £13·75
Daily Ticket £ 2·45

   a How much is the price of seven daily tickets?

   b How much money would she save buying a weekly ticket?

3. The weights of a rowing team are recorded below:

Rower A 62·5 kg   Rower B 68·4 kg   Rower C 70·9 kg   Rower D 65·6 kg

   a Calculate the total weight of the team.

   b What is the difference between the heaviest and lightest rower?

4. The Happy Haddock is a very popular fish and chip shop.

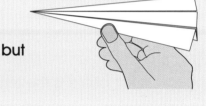

Calculate the cost of:
a 2 sausage suppers
b 5 fish suppers
c 3 pie suppers and a chicken supper
d 6 bags of chips and 4 pie suppers.
e For each of the meals above what whould be the change from £20?
f A group of six friends all ordered the same. The bill was £17·94. What meal did they buy?

Fish Supper £3·75
Sausage Supper £2·99
Chicken Supper £4·29
Pie Supper £2·55
Chips £0·85

 Challenge

Four children had a competition to see who could throw their paper darts the furthest.
The old record was 18·18 m.

Sharon threw 4·29 m short of the record.
James threw 2·17 m further than Sharon but 3·38 m shorter than Meera.
Henry threw a third further than Meera.

What distance did each person throw?

3 Adding and Subtracting with a Calculator

We can use the calculator's memory to help compare two sums.

Example
Find the difference between the total volume of red bottles and the total volume of the orange bottles.

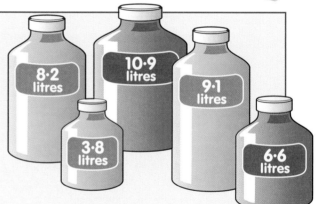

10·9 + 6·6 = 17·5
Store this in the calculator's memory

8·2 + 3·8 + 9·1 = 21·1
then 21·1 – **Recall memory** = 3·6

The difference in volume is 3·6 litres·

Estimate: 11 + 7 = 18; 8 + 4 + 9 = 21; 21 – 18 = 4
Check: 4 is close to 3·6 ✔

A

1. Calculate the difference in total volume between:

   a blue and yellow bottles
   b blue and green bottles
   c green and yellow bottles.

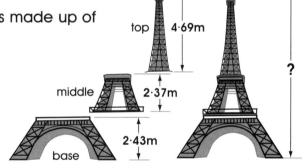

2. Calculate:

   a 136·9 + 23·7 + 0·8 + 29·3   b 78·68 − 39·79 + 26·62

3. A delivery team loads four parcels of **36·7 kg**, **78·9 kg**, **41·2 kg** and **63·5 kg** on to a van.

   a What is the weight of all the parcels?
   b What is the difference in weight between the heaviest and lightest parcel?

4. A museum's model of the Eiffel Tower is made up of three sections. Calculate:

   a the combined height of all three sections
   b the difference between the top and base sections.

   top 4·69m
   middle 2·37m
   2·43m base
   ?

5. Celine and Liam went shopping with £40 between them.

   a Who spent the most money?
   b How much more?
   c What change did they have left?

   Liam bought:
   Magazine   £2·50
   Poster   £4·99
   Phone card   £7·50

   Celine bought:
   CD   £12·99
   Metallic Pens   £4·25

Challenge

Decimal Pyramids are built in this way.
Each number above is the total of the two below.
Build these pyramids in the same way.

25·4
11·6 13·9

26·71
15·23 11·48

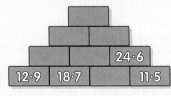
24·6
12·9 18·7 11·5

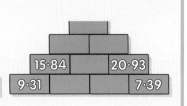
15·84 20·93
9·31 7·39

B

1. Calculate the difference between the perimeters of:

   a A and B   b A and C   c B and C

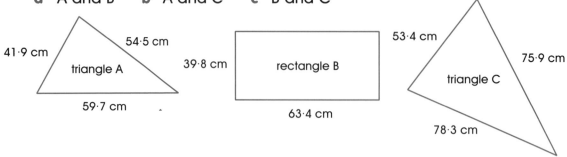

41·9 cm
54·5 cm
triangle A
59·7 cm

39·8 cm
rectangle B
63·4 cm

53·4 cm
75·9 cm
triangle C
78·3 cm

Be sure to estimate, calculate and check your answer.

2. A transit van can carry a maximum load of 1983 kg.
   Five parcels of: 80·3 kg, 97·6 kg, 55·2 kg, 67·5 kg, 91·8 kg
   have already been put on the van.

   a What is the total weight of the five parcels?
   b What weight can still be put on the van?

3. Complete:

   a 23·67 + ☐ = 59·03   b ☐ − 39·21 = 17·85

4. Sandwood Primary had a summer fayre to raise funds for charity.
   Here is the total made at four of the stalls:

Cake and
Candy
£ 35·97

Books
£ 27·63

Soak the
Teacher
£ 51

Raffle
£ 44·80

   a What was the total amount of money raised at the four stalls?
   b How much more money did the Soak the Teacher stall make than the
     Books stall?

> ## Challenge
>
> If the school raised £237·99 the previous year, how much money must the
> other stalls make to beat last year's grand total?

Challenge

Sort these cards into two equal piles so that the total of each pile is 100.

23·34 **31·96** **21·98** **24·11** **32·15** **17·28** **26·46** **22·72**

4 Multiplying and Dividing with a Calculator

Another good check with a calculator is to reverse the process.

Example   Calculate 63·9 ÷ 9

$$63·9 ÷ 9 = 7·1 \quad \text{(by calculator)}$$
check: $7·1 × 9 = 63·9$ ✔ (this guards against bad button pushing!)

A

1. What number comes out of each function machine?

   a IN   **13·7** → **× 9** → ◯ OUT   **b** IN   **463·2** → **÷ 12** → ◯ OUT

   c IN   **28·15** → **× 32** → ◯ OUT   **d** IN   **864·5** → **÷ 26** → ◯ OUT

2. Magi-Gro compost is sold in 28·5 litre bags.
   Calculate the volume of compost in:

   a 9 bags   **b** 16 bags   **c** 25 bags   **d** 40 bags

3. The Steam Express miniature train travels 3·49 km round a theme park.
   Calculate the distance travelled in:

   a 9 journeys   **b** 15 journeys   **c** 28 journeys   **d** 50 journeys

4. Three brands of crisps are sold in different sized boxes.
   Which variety of crisps is the cheapest?

   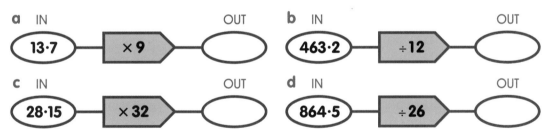

	Cost
24 packs of Frispy Crispies	£9·36
36 packs of Crunch Munch	£12·60
60 packs of Taste Invaders	£22·20

5. An 8·25 kg block of cheese is divided into 25 equal pieces and packaged for sale. What is the weight of one piece?

6. A souvenir shop has a variety of Nessie items for sale.

Calculate the cost of:
a 8 caps
b 11 tea towels
c 20 mugs
d 19 caps
e 26 tea towels
f 36 mugs
g 28 Nessie mouse pads cost £97·72. What is the cost of one mouse pad?

Remember to show your working

Challenge

Lewis spends exactly £49 buying tea towels and caps for friends and family.

How many caps and tea towels does he buy? *(Hint: he buys at least 3 of each.)*

B

1. Yasmin took advantage of a supermarket offer.

a If 12 tins of soup cost £7·08 how much did she pay for 10?
b There was another special deal on rolls.
If 2 dozen rolls cost £3·36 how much did she pay for 20?

Buy 12 tins of soup for the price of 10.

Buy 2 dozen rolls for the price of 16.

2. A farmer puts 969·6 kg of hay into bales.
Calculate the weight of each bale if the farmer divides the hay into:

a 24 bales   b 32 bales   c 48 bales

3. Squeaky Clean Car Wash uses 29·7 litres to wash one car.
   Calculate how many litres used to wash:

   a 15 cars   b 27 cars   c 60 cars

4. A 0·25 m piece of gift ribbon costs 19p.

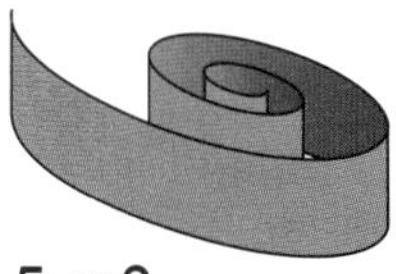

   What would be the cost of:
   a 2 m   b 10 m   c 20 m   d 15·5 m?
   e Jenny spent £5·32 on ribbon. How many metres did she buy?

Challenge

Michael keyed a number into his calculator 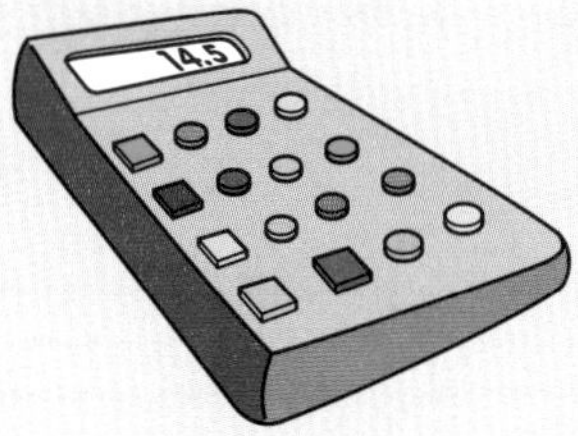
❖ He multiplied it by 25
❖ He divided the result by 18
❖ He multiplied this by 29
❖ Finally he divided his answer by 35 and got the answer 14·5

What number did Michael first key into his calculator?

Challenge

Using only these buttons on your calculator, can you make the following numbers?

| 9.4 | 1.75 |
| 0.6 | 1.68 |

2 4 7 .
× ÷ =

You can only use the ⌁ & ⌁ buttons more than once for any one number.

Unit 19   Tiling and Symmetry

Name that tune!

 1   **Looking Back**

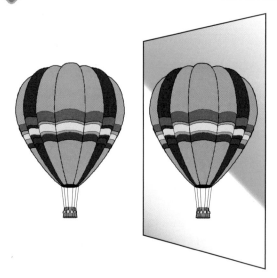

A shape has line symmetry if it looks the same when viewed in a mirror.

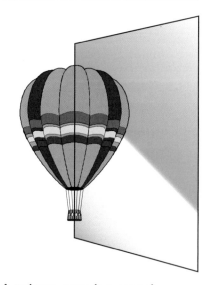

A mirror can be used to find the line, or axis, of symmetry.

A

1.   **a**   Cut out ten congruent (identically shaped) triangles. Use two colours of paper, five of each colour.
      b   Turn one set upside-down. (This will make the next step easier.)
      c   Make a tiling and glue it into your jotter.
      d   Now do the same with ten four-sided shapes.

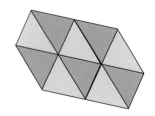

2. Copy and complete each tiling filling as much of a 10 by 10 grid as possible.

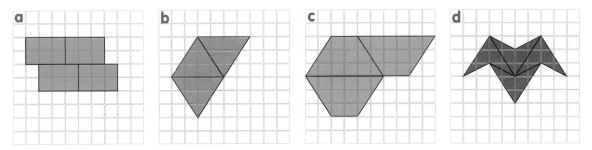

a   b   c   d

3. Follow these steps to make a symmetrical shape to stick in your jotter.

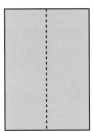  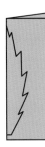  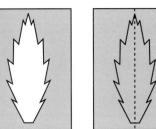 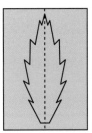

Take a sheet of paper . . .   fold in half   cut out a shape at the crease . . .   open out to reveal a symmetrical shape (a dandelion leaf) and the hole from where it came   Note that the shape will fit back into the hole in two ways

4. a Copy each shape onto squared paper.
   b Draw the line of symmetry of the shape.

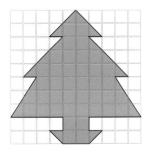 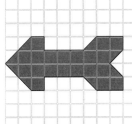 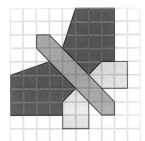 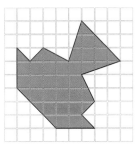

5. a Copy each shape onto squared paper.
   b Complete it to give the shape symmetry about the dotted line.

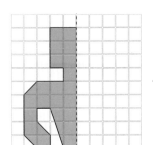 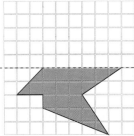 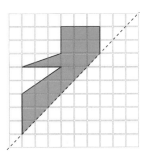 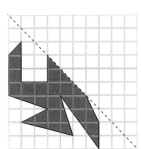

2 Making Changes

Jack of Spades

Flipped over

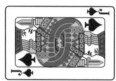
Turned through 90°

Reflected in a
vertical mirror

shrunk   squashed

You can see how the Jack of
Spades has been altered in
each case … but if the Jack
has been turned through 180°
the only way you can tell is if
you're told.

Turned through 180°

A

1. Here is the Joker of the pack.

   Describe in your own words the changes the Joker has gone
   through in each case.

a   b   c   e   f   g   h   i

d

2. What change has been made by the artist to create each pair of images?

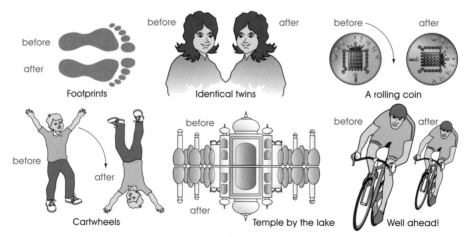

before
after
Footprints

before   after
Identical twins

before   after
A rolling coin

before
after
Cartwheels

before
after
Temple by the lake

before   after
Well ahead!

B

1. A rectangle ABCD is cut out and replaced in the hole as shown.

   a Where do points A and B end up?
   b Where do lines AB and AD end up?
   c Where do angles ∠ ABC and ∠ BCD end up?

2. An equilateral triangle is cut out, turned and placed back in the hole from which it came.

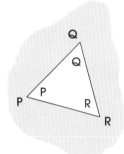 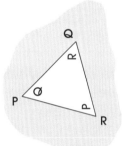

   a Where did points P and Q end up?
   b Where do lines PQ and QR end up?
   c Where do angles ∠ PQR and ∠ QRP end up?
   d If a feature ends up on top of another, then the features are equal.
      i Name a length equal to RP.
      ii Name an angle equal to ∠ RPQ.

3. Which of the following will look the same after being:

   i   reflected in a horizontal mirror
   ii reflected in a vertical mirror
   iii turned upside down.

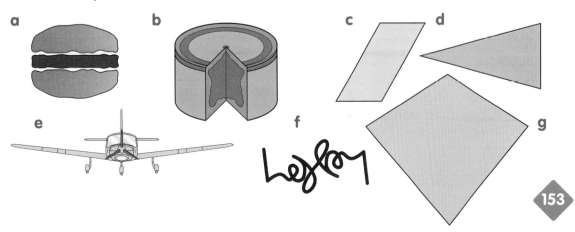

3 Lines of Symmetry

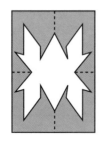

Fold a sheet of paper in half . . . and in half again
Cut a shape out of the right angle . . . and open
out to reveal a shape with two lines of symmetry.

Note that the shape will fit back into the hole from
which it came in four different ways.

A

1. The simplest of cuts produces a four-
    sided figure.

    a Make this figure.
    b Glue it into your jotter.
    c Mark on it the two lines of symmetry.
    d What kind of figure is it?

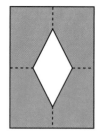

2. This pattern has been made by reflecting a pattern in a
    vertical line of symmetry and then reflecting the result in
    the horizontal line of symmetry.
    Copy and complete the following designs so that they
    have two lines of symmetry.
    [Reflect in AB and then in PQ.]

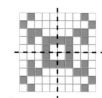

a

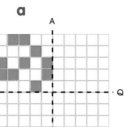

b

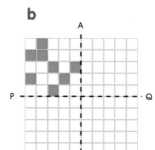

c

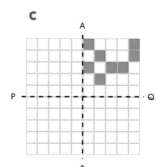

d

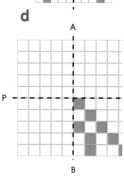

3. A rectangle has two lines of symmetry, PQ and RS.
    They cross each other at T.

    If the rectangle folds over along RS:
    a where does ∠ PTR end up?
    b what is the sum of ∠ PTR and ∠ RTQ?
    c what is the size of ∠ PTR?
    d Copy and complete the following sentence:
       If a shape has two lines of symmetry these lines cross at an angle of … .

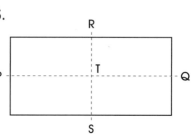

Challenge

Colour in just enough squares to give this pattern two lines of symmetry.

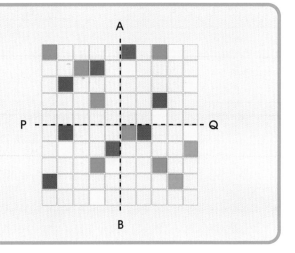

B

1.

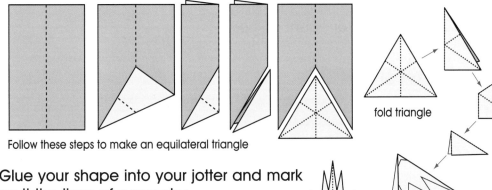

Follow these steps to make an equilateral triangle

fold triangle

a Glue your shape into your jotter and mark on it the lines of symmetry.

b Repeat the steps until you get the folded triangle.
Cut out along two lines which are at right angles to the sides.

c What kind of shape do you get?

d Glue it into your jotter and mark the lines of symmetry.

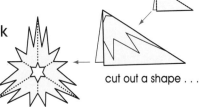

cut out a shape . . .

Open up to reveal a shape with three lines of symmetry

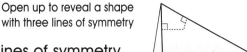

2. Start with a square of paper.

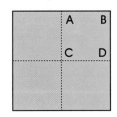   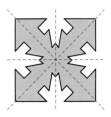

Fold in half twice ... to form ABCD.

Fold along the diagonal BC to form triangle ABC.

Cut out a pattern in the triangle.

Open out to reveal a shape with four lines of symmetry.

Glue your shape into your jotter and mark on it the four lines of symmetry.

3.

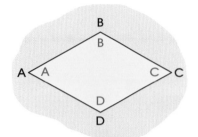 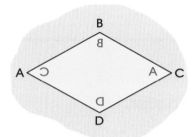

ABCD has two lines of symmetry.
If we reflect the shape in the vertical line of symmetry AB goes to BC.
So AB = CB.

a Where does AD go when the shape is reflected in the vertical line of symmetry?
b So name a line equal in length to AD.

4. In this picture the shape has been reflected in the horizontal line of symmetry.

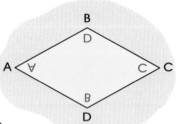

a Where does AB end up now?
b Name a line equal to AB.
c Where does ∠ABC end up when the shape is reflected in the horizontal axis?
d Name two pairs of equal angles.

 Making Tilings

 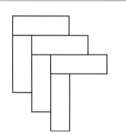 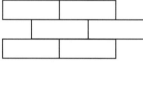

Many shapes tile.
The rectangle tiles regularly in more than one way.

1. A domino is a 2 by 1 rectangle.

Sketch three ways the domino can be tiled regularly.

2. A bee makes a honeycomb.
It looks like tiling of hexagons.

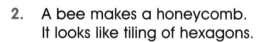

a Draw a tiling of hexagons.
You may use tracing paper.
You should show at least one tile completely surrounded by others.

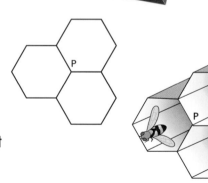

Notice that at P three angles of the hexagon fit round a point.
b How many degrees fit round a point?
c If the angles are equal, how big is each?
d Sketch a tiling that shows that each angle of a rectangle is 90°.

3. Every four-sided shape tiles.

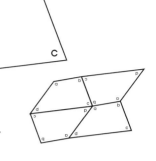

   a Look back at the previous page for help if
   needed and make a tiling of this four-sided
   figure.
   As you draw each tile, label the angles as shown.
   b Look carefully at a point where four tiles meet.
   What can be said about the sum of the angles of a four-
   sided figure?

4. If a shape tiles, it can always be altered to a new shape which also tiles.

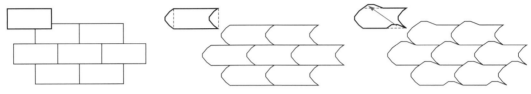

Rectangles in a brick pattern.   Cut off back and glue it to   Cut off bottom right and
                                  front ... the new shape   glue it to top left ... the
                                  tiles.   new shape tiles.

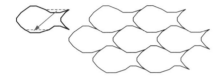   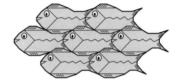

Cut off top right and glue it to   And with a bit imagination ...
bottom left ... the new shape tiles.

Trace the shape on your right
and cut and glue it as suggested
above to make a template for a
fish that tiles.

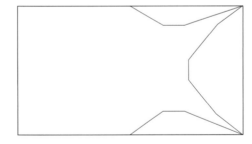

Challenge

See what you can find out
about the art of M. C. Escher
on the Internet.

See if you can design your
own picture tile.

A clowder of cats

Unit 20 Fractions

How do you halve a cake accurately?

One person cuts, the other chooses!

1 Looking Back

1. Copy and complete the following to create equivalent fractions:

   a $\dfrac{1}{3} = \dfrac{1 \times 3}{3 \times 3} = \dfrac{3}{\square}$

   b $\dfrac{2}{5} = \dfrac{2 \times 3}{5 \times 3} = \dfrac{\square}{15}$

   c $\dfrac{3}{4} = \dfrac{12}{\square}$

   d $\dfrac{4}{5} = \dfrac{12}{\square}$

   e $\dfrac{5}{6} = \dfrac{20}{\square}$

   f $\dfrac{9}{10} = \dfrac{\square}{100}$

   g $\dfrac{1}{8} = \dfrac{\square}{32}$

   h $\dfrac{7}{8} = \dfrac{49}{\square}$

   i $\dfrac{7}{10} = \dfrac{\square}{60}$

   j $\dfrac{1}{4} = \dfrac{4}{\square}$

   k $\dfrac{3}{4} = \dfrac{21}{\square}$

   l $\dfrac{2}{5} = \dfrac{\square}{80}$

2. You might halve a cake by cutting it into two equal parts. You can have the same amount of cake if you cut it into eight equal parts and take four of them.

   $$\dfrac{1}{2} = \dfrac{4}{8}$$

Simplify the following fractions:

   a $\dfrac{12}{15}$

   b $\dfrac{20}{25}$

   c $\dfrac{16}{20}$

   d $\dfrac{24}{30}$

   e $\dfrac{40}{48}$

   f $\dfrac{45}{50}$

   g $\dfrac{30}{36}$

   h $\dfrac{32}{56}$

   i $\dfrac{75}{100}$

   j $\dfrac{80}{100}$

3. There are 24 children in a class and 8 of the children wear blue socks.
   8 out of 24 wear blue socks … you can write $\frac{8}{24}$ of class wear blue socks.

   a Out of a class of 30 children 12 had sharp pencils.
      Write this as a fraction and then simplify it.

   b There are 40 children at a rugby tournament and 5 have their socks
      rolled down.
      Write this as a fraction.

   c In a class of 24 pupils 18 children get all their work correct.
      i Write this as a fraction and simplify it.
      ii What fraction got the work wrong?

   d In a school photograph of 50 children 20 are smiling. Write this as a
      simple fraction.

   e There are 300 children on a school register and 60 of these children
      were born in April. Write this as a fraction.

4. Calculate:

   a $\frac{1}{2}$ of 36   b $\frac{1}{4}$ of 64   c $\frac{1}{5}$ of 85   d $\frac{1}{6}$ of 96.
   e $\frac{1}{5}$ of 255   f $\frac{1}{8}$ of 344   g $\frac{1}{7}$ of 448   h $\frac{1}{9}$ of 252.
   i $\frac{1}{2}$ of £44   j $\frac{1}{3}$ of £81   k $\frac{1}{4}$ of £1.20   l $\frac{1}{5}$ of £2.45.
   m $\frac{1}{2}$ of 2 metres   n $\frac{1}{5}$ of 4 metres   o $\frac{1}{6}$ of 2.40 metres

5. $\frac{1}{6}$ of the children in a class of 36 were absent.
   a How many children were absent?
   b How many children were present?

6. $\frac{1}{8}$ of the cars in the staff car park were two years old.
   There are 120 cars in the car park. How many are two years old?

7. Calculate each of the following:

   a $\frac{2}{3}$ of 36   b $\frac{3}{4}$ of 36   c $\frac{5}{6}$ of 36   d $\frac{5}{9}$ of 36   e $\frac{7}{12}$ of 36
   f $\frac{2}{3}$ of 129   g $\frac{3}{4}$ of 424   h $\frac{5}{6}$ of 456   i $\frac{5}{9}$ of 378   j $\frac{7}{12}$ of 108
   k $\frac{1}{10}$ of 70   l $\frac{3}{10}$ of 240   m $\frac{7}{10}$ of 350   n $\frac{9}{10}$ of 720   o $\frac{3}{10}$ of 640

8. $\frac{7}{10}$ of the shops in town are open before school starts.
   There are 40 shops. How many are open?

9. $\frac{2}{3}$ of the children at school have green school bags.
   There are 165 children. How many have green bags?

10. There are 25 teachers in the school and $\frac{2}{5}$ of them live within five miles of
    the school. How many teachers live within five miles of the school?

2 Fractions to Decimals

Fractions can be written as decimals.

This shape is divided into ten pieces, seven are coloured.

You can write this as a common fraction $\frac{7}{10}$, or as a decimal fraction, 0·7.

A

1. a Copy the strip above and write the common fraction and the decimal
       fraction below it.
    b Draw another strip of ten pieces on squared paper and colour three
       squares. Below it write the fraction coloured as a common fraction and
       a decimal fraction.
    c Repeat the process having coloured nine squares.

2. a Draw on squared paper a 10 by 10 square.
       How many small squares make up the large square?
    b Colour 37 of the squares in blue. The fraction is $\frac{37}{100}$.
       This can be written as a decimal 0·37.
    c On the same square colour seven squares red.
       This is $\frac{7}{100}$, it means seven hundredths and as a decimal is written 0·07.

3. Change each decimal fraction into a common fraction:

    a 0·7   b 0·71   c 0·07   d 0·70   e 0·17

4. Change each decimal fraction into a common fraction and make it as
    simple as you can:

    a 0·06   b 0·15   c 0·2   d 0·20   e 0·80

5. Calculate: a 0·25 of £80   b $\frac{1}{4}$ of £80.

    c What do we mean when we say 0·25 is equivalent to $\frac{1}{4}$?

6. a Draw another 10 by 10 square and colour in 15 squares blue.
    b What fraction are coloured?
       Write this as a common fraction and as a decimal fraction.
    c Colour another 34 of the squares red.
    d Write the fraction coloured red as both a common and a decimal
       fraction.
    e Now colour 45 squares green and say what fraction is green.
    f How many squares are not coloured. Can you write this as a decimal?

7. Write the following fractions as decimals:

Remember
that $\frac{1}{100}$ is written as 0·01

a $\frac{13}{100}$ b $\frac{23}{100}$ c $\frac{54}{100}$ d $\frac{3}{10}$ e $\frac{7}{10}$ f $\frac{50}{100}$ g $\frac{40}{100}$

8. 100 pence makes £1. When we have 70p we have $\frac{70}{100}$ of a pound which is written as £0·70.

Write the following amounts of money as common fractions and then as decimal fractions of a pound (£):

a	34p	b	45p	c	56p	d	9p	e	80p
f	15p	g	82p	h	50p	i	29p	j	5p

9. A boy spends 72 pence on a pencil and a ruler.
   Write this both as a common and as a decimal fraction of a pound (£).

10. **100 centimetres make a metre, so a centimetre is $\frac{1}{100}$ of a metre.**
    Write the following lengths both as a common and as a decimal fraction of a metre:

a	92 cm	b	36 cm	c	42 cm	d	60 cm	e	15 cm
f	4 cm	g	27 cm	h	81 cm	i	3 cm	j	75 cm

3 Percentages to Fractions

Look at the label on this sweatshirt. It tells you what the garment is made from.

If all the shirt is being described then the parts should add up to 100% …

50% + 25% + 25% = 100%

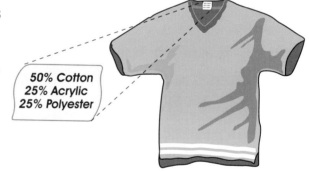

50% Cotton
25% Acrylic
25% Polyester

1. a Draw a 10 by 10 square and colour 25 of the squares red.
      Colour 40 of the squares green and 35 of the squares blue.
   b Copy and complete this chart:
   c Check that all is shaded …
      $\frac{100}{100} = 1 = 100\%$.

Red squares	$\frac{25}{100}$	25%
Green squares	$\frac{40}{100}$	
Blue squares		
Total shaded		

2. Copy and complete these tables. Remember the whole always adds up to 100%.

a

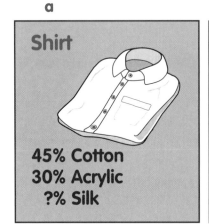

Shirt

45% Cotton
30% Acrylic
?% Silk

b

Chocolate Rabbit

20% Cocoa
30% Sugar
?% Milk

c

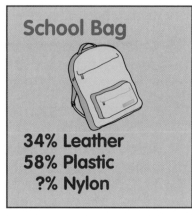

School Bag

34% Leather
58% Plastic
?% Nylon

3. Change these percentages to common fractions:
   a 25% b 20% c 10% d 75%
   e 40% f 80% g 60% h 70%

4. a 25% of the children in the school have school lunches.
      Write this as a common fraction in its simplest form.
   b 50% of the jotters in the school cupboard are blue.
      Write this as a common fraction.
   c 10% of the children in the school wear brown shoes. What fraction wear
      brown shoes? What fraction do not?

5. Calculate each set and complete the sentence.

   a 25% of 24   b 25% of 48   c 25% of 84
   ✤ Copy this statement: **Finding 25% is the same as finding a quarter.**

6. a 10% of 50   b 10% of 150   c 10% of 240
   ✤ Copy this statement: **Finding 10% is the same as finding a tenth.**

7. a 20% of 25   b 20% of 45   c 20% of 125
   ✤ Copy this statement: **Finding 20% is the same as finding a ....**

8. a 50% of 60   b 50% of 36   c 50% of 120
   ✤ Copy this statement: **Finding 50% is the same as finding a ....**

9. a 1% of 700   b 1% of 2300
   ✤ Copy this statement: **Finding 1% is the same as finding a ....**

10. a 100% of 45   b 100% of 650   c 100% of 3450
    ✤ Copy this statement: **Finding 100% is the same as finding a ....**

11. Find:

a 75% of 24	b 25% of 160	c 40% of 50		d 60% of 90
e 80% of 60	f 70% of 140	g 30% of 120		

B

1. In a school 120 pupils are asked some questions.

   a 25% of the pupils have woolly hats. How many have woolly hats?

   b 10% of the pupils come to school by bus. How many children is this?

   c 20% of the pupils go home for lunch. How many go home for lunch?

   d 50% of the pupils live to the west of the school. How many children live to the west of the school?

   e 80% of the children love maths. How many children love maths?

2.

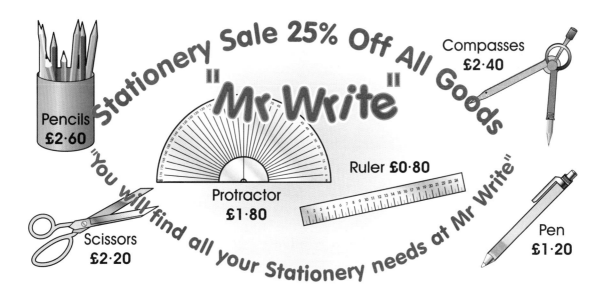

There is 25% off all the goods in the shop. The shopkeeper is giving a discount.

Example: A rubber usually costs £0.60. 25% of 60 = 15.
The shopkeeper takes 15p off the price.
The sale price of the rubber is now £0·45.

   a Work out **how much he takes off** each item in the shop.

   b Write out the sale prices of the items.

4 Percentages to Decimals

Example 1
Express 25% as a decimal fraction.
$25\% = \frac{25}{100} = 25 \div 100 = 0.25$

Example 2
Find 23% of £4·00.
$23\% = 0.23$
So 23% of £4·00 = 0·23 × 4 = £0·92.

A

1. Change the following percentages into decimals:

a 25%	b 10%	c 40%	d 5%	e 8%	f 75%
g 72%	h 56%	i 44%	j 90%	k 100%	l 1%

2. Convert the following to decimal fractions then evaluate:

a 27% of £45	b 42% of £660	c 28% of £536
d 7% of 250 m	e 67% of 1250 km	f 8% of 2340

3. a 80 metres of material was ordered to make curtains for the classrooms.
      It was found that 36% of the material was flawed.
      How much material was flawed?

   b The company agreed to take 17% off the price. The original price was
      £640.
      ✤ How much money is this discount?
      ✤ How much will the school now need to pay?

4. To paint the school, 235 litres of paint were ordered at a cost of £2350.
   As this was a large order the company agreed to take 4% off the price.

   a How much was the discount?
   b With this discount, how much did the school pay?

5. Children in a school took part in a survey. 128 children answered
   questions and the results were expressed in percentages.

   a 27% of the children said they enjoyed walking. How many children
      liked walking?
   b 66% said they liked playing ball games. How many
      liked ball games?
   c 87% said they enjoyed maths. How many liked
      maths?
   d 96% said they could not live without TV. How many
      had to have a TV?
   e 4% said they never watched TV. How many never
      watched TV?

5 Fractions, Decimals, Percentages

1. Copy and complete the table.

Percentage	25%	20%			30%			
Decimal	0·25		0·10			0·36		0·95
Fraction	$\frac{1}{4}$			$\frac{3}{4}$			$\frac{3}{20}$	

2. Look at Robin's exam results.

   a Convert all his results into percentages. You can use a calculator.

Name	Robin Goodfellow					
Subject	History	Geography	Maths	English	Science	RE
Mark	$\frac{23}{25}$	$\frac{17}{20}$	$\frac{46}{50}$	$\frac{9}{10}$	$\frac{38}{40}$	$\frac{89}{100}$
Decimal						
Percentage						

Now that the results are all expressed as percentages we can compare them.

   b What was Robin's best subject?
   c What was his worst?
   d List his subjects in order, from best to worst performance.

Challenge

All the classes in the school were asked what improvements they wanted to the school.

To help the headteacher make a decision each class gave her information about the one improvement most of their class voted for.

As these were all expressed as fractions or decimals the headteacher converted them into percentages before she made her decision.

   ❖ $\frac{15}{24}$ children in P4 wanted new carpets.
   ❖ 0·84 children in P5 wanted the classrooms to be painted.
   ❖ $\frac{17}{20}$ in P6 wanted new desks.
   ❖ 0·8 in P7 wanted a store cupboard for the gym.

Draw a table like the one in question 2 and complete with the information above.

What decision do you think the headteacher made?

Unit 21 Time and Temperature

1 Looking Back

1. Match up each time with a display.

   a 21:30
   b Half past 4 in the afternoon
   c 18:10
   d Half past 4 in the morning
   e 10 past 6 in the morning
   f 14:30

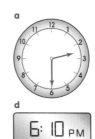

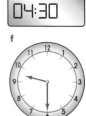

2. Copy and complete the missing times:

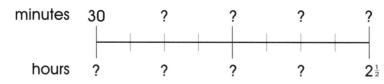

   minutes 30   ?   ?   ?   ?

   hours   ?   ?   ?   ? $2\frac{1}{2}$

3. Change:

   a 9 a.m. to 24-hour time
   b 15:20 to 12-hour time
   c 12 noon to 24-hour time
   d 2.47 p.m. to 24-hour time

4. a Which of A or B shows the highest temperature?
   b What is the temperature shown on A?
   c What is the difference in temperature between A and B?

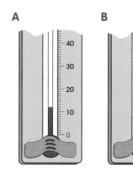

5. a When does the restaurant close on Sunday?

    b For how long is the restaurant open on Tuesday?

    c How long is the restaurant open for during the course of one week?

Restaurant	Daytime	Evening
Monday	CLOSED	CLOSED
Tuesday	CLOSED	6 pm - 9 pm
Wednesday	CLOSED	6 pm - 9 pm
Thursday	CLOSED	6 pm - 9 pm
Friday	12 noon - 2 pm	6 pm - 9:30 pm
Saturday	12:30 pm - 2:30 pm	6 pm - 9:30 pm
Sunday	12 noon - 3 pm	CLOSED

2 How Long?

A museum opens at 10.45 a.m. and closes at 2.10 p.m. For how long is it open?

Use the time line

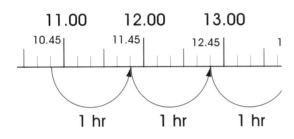

Method 2: subtract

1. How long is it from:

    a 02:00 to 07:15   b 10:30 to 14:40   c 07:45 to 10:40
    d 11:48 to 18:22   e 12:00 to 00:10   f 23:00 to 03:15
    g 19:24 to 01:50   h 22:35 to 02:12   i 04:13 to 02:05

2. Complete the table of television times:

	Starts	Lasts	Finishes
programme a	15:50	1 hr 20 min	?
programme b	18:35	?	20:50
programme c	?	3 hr 25 min	18:00
programme d	11:25	45 min	?
programme e	10:35	?	12:10
programme f	?	2 hr 18 min	01:40

3. At the Multiplex Film Centre:

    a *Johnny English*: Showing at 18:40. Film lasts 88 min.
    When does it finish?

    b *The Jungle Book 2*: Finishes at 18:25. Film lasts 72 min.
    When does it start?

    c *The Little Polar Bear*: Showing at 14:50, finishing at 16:07.
    How long does the film last in minutes?

3 ◆ Timetables

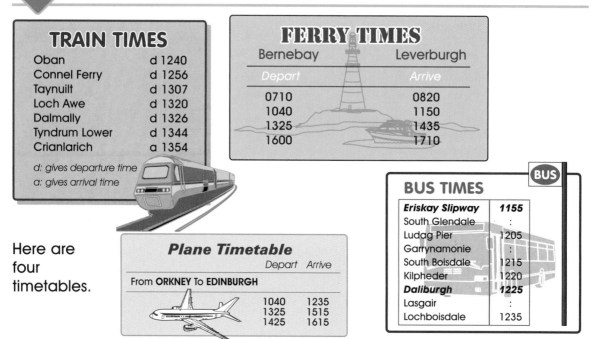

TRAIN TIMES

Oban	d 1240
Connel Ferry	d 1256
Taynuilt	d 1307
Loch Awe	d 1320
Dalmally	d 1326
Tyndrum Lower	d 1344
Crianlarich	a 1354

d: gives departure time
a: gives arrival time

FERRY TIMES

Bernebay	Leverburgh
Depart	Arrive
0710	0820
1040	1150
1325	1435
1600	1710

Plane Timetable

From **ORKNEY** To **EDINBURGH**

Depart	Arrive
1040	1235
1325	1515
1425	1615

BUS TIMES

Eriskay Slipway	1155
South Glendale	:
Ludag Pier	1205
Garrynamonie	:
South Boisdale	1215
Kilpheder	1220
Daliburgh	1225
Lasgair	:
Lochboisdale	1235

Here are
four
timetables.

1. **a** When does the train leave
    Oban?
    b When does the bus arrive in
    Lochboisdale?
    c When does the last ferry leave
    Bernebay?
    d When does the first plane arrive
    in Edinburgh?
    e Where is the train at 13:20?
    f Where is the bus at 12:15?

2. **a** How long does the ferry take?
    b How long does the train take
    from Oban to Crianlarich?
    c How long does the bus take
    from Eriskay to Lochboisdale?
    d How long is the first flight?
    e How long are the other flights?

3. a Iain arrives at the airport at 2.30 p.m. Is he in time for the last flight?

   b Diane arrives in Edinburgh at 15:15 on a flight from Orkney. When did she leave Orkney?

   c Fiona gets on the Lochboisdale Bus at 12:15. Where is she?

4. a It is 11 a.m. Graeme is on the Edinburgh flight from Orkney. How long is it since the flight started?

   b Rowena takes the train from the Connel Ferry to Crianlarich. How long does it take?

   c How long does the bus take from Ludag Pier to South Boisdale?

5. One ferry sails to and fro between Tobermory and Kilchoan all day.

TOBERMORY – KILCHOAN

| | TOBERMORY | KILCHOAN | KILCHOAN | TOBERMORY |
	Depart	Arrive	Depart	Arrive
MON – SAT	0720	0755	0805	0840
	0930	1005	1015	1050
	1100	1135	1145	1220
	1300	1335	1345	1420
	1430	1505	1515	1550
	1600	1635	1645	1720
	1800	1835	1845	1920

   a When in the morning does it first sail?
   b When does it stop sailing at the end of the day?
   c How long does the **return** journey take from Tobermory?
   d Hannah arrives in Tobermory at 9 a.m. When is the next ferry to Kilchoan?
   e Sarah is in Kilchoan and has to be in Tobermory by 6 p.m. What is the latest ferry she can catch?

B

Letter codes appear on some timetables. This warns you that there is something different about the information. You should carefully read what the code means.

FERRY TIMES

| | ARDROSSAN | BRODICK | BRODICK | ARDROSSAN |
	Depart	Arrive	Depart	Arrive
MON – SAT	0700	0755	0820	0915
	0945	1040	1105	1200
	1230	1325	1350	1445
	1515	1610	1640	1735
	1800	1855	1920	2015
	2030 A	2125 A	2140 A	2235 A
SUNDAY	0945	1040	1105	1200
	1230	1325	1350	1445
	1515	1610	1640	1735
	1800	1855	1920	2015

CODE A Fridays only.

169

1. How many ferries leave Ardrossan for Brodick on:
   a Monday   **b** Friday   **c** Sunday?
   d On Sunday when does the first ferry leave Ardrossan?
   e On Friday when does the last ferry leave Brodick?
   f How long does the ferry take for one journey?
   Hamish arrives in Brodick on Saturday at 8 a.m. He wants to spend the day in Ardrossan but must be back in Brodick by 6 p.m.
   g Work out which ferries he gets and how long he can stay in Brodick.
   h Could he have done the same on a Sunday? Explain.

2. Trains sometimes don't stop at stations. If a time is missing in the table then the train doesn't stop!

   ### Sunday Train Times

Edinburgh	0855	0915	0935	0942	- - - -	1055	1115	1145
Haymarket	0900	0919	0939	0946	- - - -	1059	1119	1149
Inverkeithing	0916	0940	0955	1003	- - - -	1115	1140	1206
Kirkcaldy	0933	1002	1011	1018	- - - -	1131	1202	1221
Markinch	- - - -	1011	- - - -	1027	- - - -	- - - -	1211	- - - -
Ladybank	- - - -	1019	- - - -	- - - -	- - - -	- - - -	1219	- - - -
Perth	- - - -	- - - -	1049	- - - -	1046	- - - -	- - - -	- - - -
Springfield	- - - -	- - - -						
Cupar	- - - -	1026		1039	- - - -	- - - -	1226	1238
Leuchars	0957	1033		1046	- - - -	1155	1233	1245
Dundee	1011	1048		1101	1111	1208	1248	1259

   On Sunday morning how many trains run from:
   a Edinburgh to Kirkcaldy   **b** Edinburgh to Markinch
   c Edinburgh to Dundee   **d** Perth to Dundee?
   e Michael got the 09:42 for Dundee but got off at Cupar by mistake. Not to worry: he hopped on the next train for Dundee.
   When did he arrive in Dundee?
   f Which train takes least time from Edinburgh to Dundee?

4   Perfect Timing

Stopwatches are used to time events. Here are two different types.

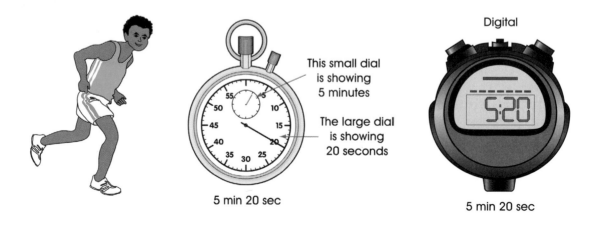

This small dial is showing 5 minutes

The large dial is showing 20 seconds

5 min 20 sec

Digital

5 min 20 sec

A

1. Write down the times, in minutes and seconds, shown on these stopwatches:

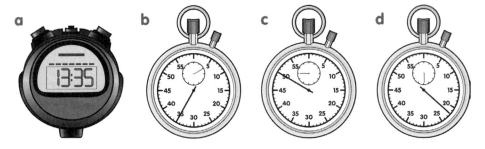

a   b   c   d

2. These stopwatches below show the times of runners in a race.

   a   Put the runners in order 1st, 2nd, 3rd and 4th.
   b   By how many seconds did the winner win?

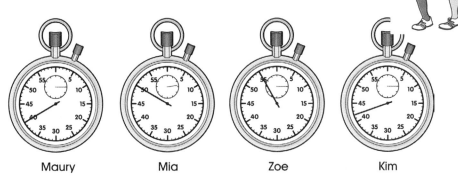

   Maury   Mia   Zoe   Kim

3. This stopwatch shows the winning time in a race.

   The gaps between each runner and the next as
   they finished were:
   3 sec, 12 sec, 1 sec and 1 min 23 sec.

   Calculate the time of each of the other four runners
   in the race.

5 Temperature

1. Write down the reading on each thermometer.

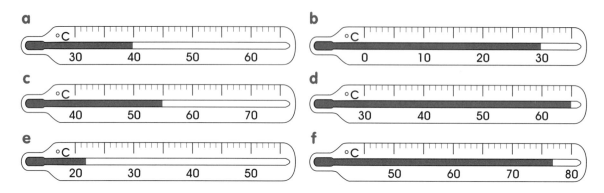

2. Arrange these thermometers in order, lowest temperature to highest:

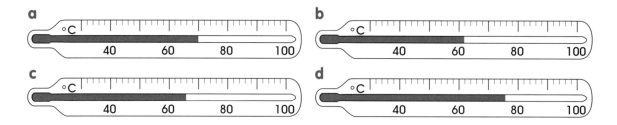

What is the difference in temperature between the lowest and the highest reading?

1. Write down the temperature readings from each of these dials:

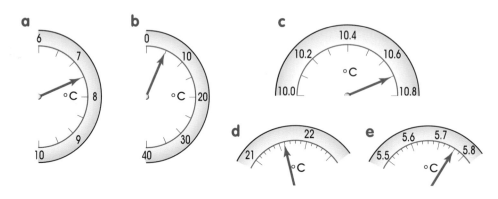

2. This table shows the percentage of seeds that germinate (sprout) at various soil temperatures.

	Soil Temperature								
	0°C	5°C	10°C	15°C	20°C	25°C	30°C	35°C	40°C
Lima Beans	0%	0%	1%	52%	82%	90%	88%	2%	0%
Celery	0%	72%	75%	80%	97%	65%	0%	0%	0%
Spinach	83%	96%	91%	82%	52%	28%	12%	0%	0%
Eggplant	0%	0%	0%	0%	21%	53%	60%	0%	0%

a Which plant needs a temperature of 20° or over to sprout?

b Each type of seed has its own 'optimum' temperature. This is the temperature at which most seeds sprout. Find the 'optimum' temperature for each type of seed.

c I plant 100 seeds of each type. At which soil temperature would I expect to get the most seeds sprouting?

Investigate

Hot and Cold Records

The highest temperature ever recorded in Scotland was 32.8°C at Dumfires on 2 July 1908.

The lowest ever recorded was –27.2°C at Braemar (Aberdeenshire) on 11 February 1895.

What is the difference between these two extreme temperatures?

Search the Internet for more temperature records and compare them with those of Scotland.

Whole Numbers

Unit 22

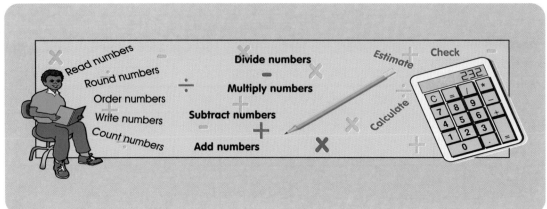

Read numbers
Round numbers
Order numbers
Write numbers
Count numbers

Divide numbers
Multiply numbers
Subtract numbers
Add numbers

Estimate   Check

Calculate

1 Looking Back

1. Copy and complete the table.

	Problem	Estimate	Calculate	Check 1 (round)	Check 2 (reverse)
a	3271 + 5826	3000 + 6000 = 9000	9097	9097 close to 9000	9097 − 3271 = 5826
b	7969 ÷ 13	8000 ÷ 10 = 800	613	613 close to 800	613 × 13 = 7969
c	1924 + 4138				
d	8051 ÷ 97				
e	6892 − 2178				
f	5126 × 12				
g	3167 + 5918				
h	5263 − 3934				
i	7362 × 98				

2. Use a calculator to find the value of each of the following. Remember to check each answer.

a
```
  5826
  3681
   714
  9216
  3628
    58
   471
+ 7582
```

b
```
   348
  7469
     5
  5134
  6317
   837
  9014
+   36
```

c 7824 − 2078 − 374 − 1709 − 2651

d 9326 − 484 − 3720 − 2875 − 97

e 23 × 14 × 25 × 52

f Multiply the first six odd numbers.

2 Picking Numbers Out of the Air

A

1. Last month 87 362 passengers used
Caledonia Airport.
Two months ago the figure was 106 540.
Last year the total number of passengers
using the airport was 740 305.

Write down these three figures in words.

2. Round each number in question 1 to:

a the nearest hundred   b the nearest thousand.

3. a The record number of passengers in a month passing through the
airport is *one hundred and ninety thousand, six hundred and eighty*.
b The record number for a year is *eight hundred and five thousand, two
hundred and seventy-five*.
Write both numbers in figures.

4. The table shows the number of people flying from Caledonia Airport to
some of the most popular places.

a Re-write the table in order,
starting with the most popular
country visited.
b Round each number to the
nearest thousand.

Country	Number
France	42 766
Spain	43 055
USA	40 687
Italy	39 820
Spanish Islands	42 498
Greece	42 805

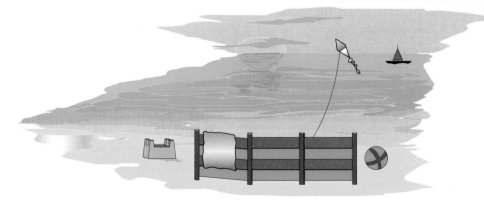

5. The table shows the number of passengers using the airport each month during 2003.
    The table also shows how this number changed in 2004.

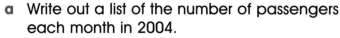

Passenger Numbers						
Year	Jan	Feb	Mar	Apr	May	Jun
2003	23 695	19 027	24 689	41 005	33 605	59 781
2004	10 more	30 less	20 more	100 less	400 more	300 more
	Jul	Aug	Sept	Oct	Nov	Dec
2003	90 050	88 583	34 095	20 946	17 892	29 984
2004	1000 less	2000 more	100 less	1000 less	200 more	100 more

a   Write out a list of the number of passengers each month in 2004.

b   Round the 2003 figures to the nearest 100.

 B

1. The luggage on a flight to Majorca weighs a total of 6382 kg.
    The passengers weigh a total of 9255 kg.

    a   What is the difference between the passengers' weight and the weight of the luggage?
    b   What is the combined weight of the luggage and passengers?

2. A return ticket from Caledonia to Sydney, Australia costs £1485.

    a   How much does it cost a party of seven to make a return trip between Caledonia and Sydney?
    b   Last year it cost £9765 for seven return tickets to Sydney.
        How much did one ticket cost last year?

3. There are three runways at Caledonia Airport.
    Their lengths are 3473 metres, 3185 metres and 1956 metres.

    a   What is the total length of the three runways combined?
    b   What is the difference in length between the longest and the shortest runways?

4. a Last year 1837 flights took off from
       Caledonia.
       1258 left on time. The rest were delayed.
       How many flights were delayed?
    b 1913 flights landed at the airport.
       985 of them landed on time.
       How many of them were late?
    c How many flights in total last year took off
       from or landed at Caledonia Airport?
    d How many of this number of flights were on
       time?

5. Paul flew from Caledonia to Cairo and then on to Johannesburg.

    a How much further was the second flight?
    b What was the total distance of the two flights?

Caledonia Airport

2587 miles
6 hours

Cairo

4012 miles
9 hours

Johannesburg

    c Divide the distance between Caledonia and
       Cairo by the time of the flight to find the
       average speed in miles per hour.
       Give your answer rounded to the nearest 10
       mph.
    d In the same way find the average speed of
       the flight from Cairo to Johannesburg.
    e In one month a pilot made six return flights
       between Caledonia and Cairo.
       What was the total mileage of these six flights?

6. The table shows the number of items sold by the airport shop last summer.

Item	Number sold
Sunglasses	2764 pairs
Cameras	1458
Sun cream	3692 bottles
After sun	874 bottles

Sunglasses
£9 a pair

£6 each

Disposable
Cameras

Sun cream
£7 a bottle

After sun
£8 a bottle

How much money was made from the sale of:
a Sunglasses   b Cameras   c Sun cream   d After sun?

e How much more money was made from the sale of disposable
   cameras than from the sale of after sun?

1. **a** On a flight to Paris the only seats occupied by passengers are the ones numbered 005 to 163.
   How many passengers are on the flight to Paris?

   b A plane flying to Majorca has 200 passenger seats. The seats numbered 1–6, 14–22, 47–89, 96–154 and 165–191 are all occupied.
   All the other passenger seats are empty.
   How many empty passenger seats are there on the plane?

 3 **On the Button**

It is good practice when using a calculator to:

❖ **estimate** then **calculate** then **check**.

 A

1. An aircraft takes off with 203 500 litres of fuel.
   When it lands it has 37 800 litres of fuel left.
   How much fuel did it use on its journey?

2. The maximum weight for a Jumbo Jet at take-off is 396 800 kilograms.
   Its maximum weight for landing is 285 900 kilograms.
   What is the difference between these two weights?

3. On a long-distance flight, 3762 coffees, 1096 teas and 1874 soft drinks were served.
   How many drinks were served altogether?

4. Each passenger's luggage must weigh no more than 35 kilograms.
   There are 412 passengers on board a flight, each with the maximum weight of luggage.
   What is the total weight of luggage?

5. To park overnight in the short-stay car park at Caledonia costs £6.
   To park for more than 24 hours in the long-stay car park costs £23.

   a One week 7934 cars used the short-stay car park.
   How much money was paid in parking fees?

   b During the same week 4765 cars used the long-stay car park.
   How much was paid in parking fees at this car park?

   c How much was collected altogether in parking fees that week?

6. Cass flies on business from Caledonia to Washington and then to Buenos Aires before flying back to Caledonia.

Caledonia Airport

3762 miles
8 hours

Washington

6097 miles
11 hours

7346 miles
17 hours

Buenos Aires

   a   How far did Cass fly altogether?
   b   Divide the distance of the flight to Washington by the time it took, to calculate the average speed of the flight in miles per hour.
   c   Calculate the average speed of the flight from:

      i   Washington to Buenos Aires
      ii Buenos Aires to Caledonia.

7. Last year the gift shop at Caledonia Airport made the sales of perfume shown in the table.

Make of perfume	Misty	Liberty	Success	Vin Eagar
Number of bottles	4695	5264	3608	923
Price per bottle	£29	£37	£43	£12

   a   How many bottles of perfume were sold?
   b   How much money was made from the sale of Liberty?
   c   How much money was made from the sale of Vin Eager?
   d   How much money was made altogether from the sale of perfume?

Challenge

An aircraft takes off from Caledonia Airport. It reaches a height of 16 000 feet after one minute.
One minute later it has climbed another 8000 feet.
Another minute later it has climbed a further 4000 feet.
One minute later it has climbed another 2000 feet.

The pilot decides to continue this pattern until the plane is at its required height of 32 000 feet.

How many minutes will it take the plane to reach the height of 32 000 feet?

Unit 23 Letters and Number Patterns

What is the address that has fallen off?

1 Looking Back

A number has fallen off the door. We can guess what it is because the numbers form a pattern, or **sequence**.
Each **term** is two more than the term before it.

5, 7, 9 __, 13   The missing term is 11.

1. Here are some simple patterns.
    Find the next four terms in each.

    a 2, 4, 6, 8, …   **b** 1, 3, 5, 7, …   **c** 5, 10, 15, 20, …
    d 7, 14, 21, 28, …   **e** 80, 72, 64, 56, …   **f** 40, 36, 32, 28, …

2. $a = 4$ and $b = 7$. Find the value of:

    a $2a$ **b** $b + 2$ **c** $8b$ **d** $a - 3$ **e** $12a$

3. Solve these equations:

    a $x + 3 = 7$ **b** $5y = 30$ **c** $t - 8 = 10$ **d** $9x = 63$

4. Find the value of the letter in each of these 'number machines':

    a IN 5 ×9 OUT y   **b** IN y ×9 OUT 63   **c** IN 4 ×W OUT 60

5. Describe the rule that changes the red numbers into the blue numbers for each set:

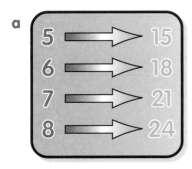 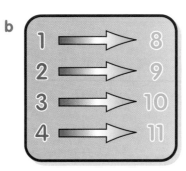 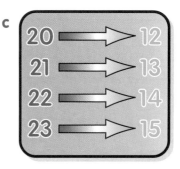

6. The *Goldilocks Buttercup* has only three petals. Copy and complete this table.

Number of flowers	1	2	3	4	5	6
Number of petals	3					

2 What's the Next Term?

1, 2, 3, … What's the next term?

1, 2, 3, 4, … Why?

Because you add 1 to a term to get the next

1, 4, 16, … What's the next term?

1, 4, 16, 64, … Why?

Because you multiply a term by 4 to get the next

Here Meg and Pete have come up with an answer based on a simple rule they have spotted.

In each case the rule tells you how to get the next term from the previous one. We talk of this as a simple **Next Term** rule.

In the following exercise we are working with simple **Next Term** rules.

1. In each case, what is the next term and why?

    a 1, 3, 5, □   **b** 5, 8, 11, □   **c** 7, 12, 17, □
    d 2, 9, 16, □   **e** 4, 14, 24, □   **f** 8, 20, 32, □

2. Match each sequence to one of the rules.

Sequences			
A	1, 3, 5 ...	1	multiply the previous term by 3
B	64, 32, 16 ...	2	double the previous term
C	1, 2, 4 ...	3	add 3 to the previous term
D	1, 4, 7 ...	4	halve the previous term
E	1, 3, 9 ...	5	add 2 to the previous term

3. Describe a simple 'next term' rule for these sequences:

    a 3, 5, 7, 9, 11, ...   **b** 15, 12, 9, 6, ...   **c** 3, 6, 12, 24, 48, ...
    d 3, 6, 9, 12, 15, ...   **e** 2, 6, 10, 14, 18, ...   **f** 2, 4, 8, 16, ...
    g 1, 4, 16, 64, 256, ...   **h** 20, 18, 16, 14, ...   **i** 3, 15, 27, 39, ...

4. List the first five terms of each sequence in the table.

	First term	Simple 'next term' rule
a	3	add 5 to the previous term
b	1	add 6 to the previous term
c	48	subtract 3 from the previous term
d	3	multiply the previous term by 4
e	7	double the previous term
f	37	subtract 6 from the previous term

5. Find the next three terms for these sequences.
    Give the simple 'next term' rule that you used.

    a 3, 6, 9, 12, 15, ...   **b** 7, 14, 28, 56, ...   **c** 70, 66, 62, 58, ...
    d 1, 10, 19, 28, ...   **e** 2, 6, 18, 54, ...   **f** 3, 6, 12, 24, ...

Less simple rule

In 1202 AD a man called Leonardo Fibonacci wrote a book which contained a puzzle that dealt with the sequence

1, 1, 2, 3, 5, 8, 13, …

the terms of this sequence are called **Fibonacci numbers** after Leonardo.

… and the 'next term' rule?: **To get any term we add the two previous terms.**

So the next term after 13 is 8 + 13 = 21

1. a Continue the sequence shown above to find the first 15 Fibonacci numbers.
    b Which of the following are Fibonacci numbers?
       90   144   378   610   987

2. We can create similar sequences by using the rule but starting with a different two terms.
    Find the first five terms of each of the 'Fibonacci-type' sequences which start with:

    a 1, 4, …   b 3, 4, …   c 2, 7, …

3. Find the next three terms of each of these sequences:

    a 2, 6, 8, 14, …   b 3, 5, 8, 13, …
    c 1, 7, 8, 15, …   d 1, 11, 12, 23, …

4. Which of the following are Fibonacci-type sequences?

    a 1, 2, 3, 4, …   b 1, 2, 3, 5, …
    c 2, 4, 6, 8, …   d 2, 4, 6, 10, …

5. Find the next two terms in each of the following sequences.
    Some are Fibonacci types and some are not. State the 'next term' rule used.

    a 2, 9, 16, 23, …   b 7, 14, 21, 35, …   c 6, 12, 18, 24, …
    d 5, 10, 20, 40, …   e 8, 16, 24, 40, …   f 625, 125, 25, …

6. 1, 1, 1, 3, 5, 9, ...   Here the rule is 'add the three previous terms to get the next.'

    a   What are the next four terms of this sequence?
        Find the rule and the next three terms of each of these:
    b   1, 1, 1, 1, 4, 7, 13, ...
    c   1, 2, 3, 6, 11, 20, ...
    d   5, 4, 3, 12, 19, ...

Challenge

A French mathematician call Blaise Pascal studied this triangular pattern.
It is called 'Pascal's triangle' after him.

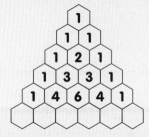

a   Each row is made from the previous row by a simple rule.
    Can you spot it?

b   Here a set of parallel lines have been drawn on the triangle.
    Calculate the sum of the terms cut by each line.
    What do you notice?

---

3   New Lists for Old

Careful: We now have two types of rules:
   ❖ A 'list changing' rule ... for turning one list into another.
   ❖ A 'next term' rule ... for working out the next term.

Example

List C:	1	2	3	4
List D:	7	14	21	28

List changing rule   … multiply each term of C by 7 to get D.

Next term rule for list D   … add 7 to the previous term.

1. Copy each table. Use the 'list changing' rule given to create list B:

a

List A:	1	2	3	4
List B:				

Double each term of list A

b

List A:	4	5	6	7
List B:				

Subtract 3 from each term of list A

c

List A:	10	20	30	40
List B:				

Add 7 to each term of list A

d

List A:	1	2	3	4
List B:				

Multiply each term of list A by 6

e

List A:	3	4	5	6
List B:				

Multiply each term of list A by 9

f

List A:	2	6	10	14
List B:				

Divide each term of list A by 2

2. Describe the 'list changing' rule to create list B from list A:

a

List A:	1	2	3	4
List B:	12	13	14	15

b

List A:	1	2	3	4
List B:	8	16	24	32

c

List A:	6	7	8	9
List B:	1	2	3	4

d

List A:	5	6	7	8
List B:	3	4	5	6

e

List A:	10	11	12	13
List B:	20	22	24	26

f

List A:	1	2	3	4
List B:	0.5	1	1.5	2

3. **a** Use the rule 'multiply by 4' to create List D from List C.

   b Describe the 'Next term' rule for List D.

   c Use the rule: 'add 14' to create List E from List C.

   d Describe the 'Next term' rule for List E.

List C:	1	2	3	4	5
List D:					
List E:					

Some two-step rules

List A:	1	2	3	4
List B:				

Example

Use the 'list changing' rule
Multiply by 3 then add 2 to create list B.

Answer

List A:	1	2	3	4
List B:	5	8	11	14

1. For each table, copy and complete using the given 'list changing' rule and then state the 'next term' rule for list B.

a

List A:	1	2	3	4
List B:				

Multiply by 6 then subtract 1.

b

List A:	1	2	3	4
List B:				

Multiply by 2 then add 3.

c

List A:	1	2	3	4
List B:				

Multiply by 8 then add 2.

d

List A:	1	2	3	4
List B:				

Multiply by 5 then subtract 4.

e

List A:	1	2	3	4
List B:				

Multiply by 10 then subtract 7.

f

List A:	1	2	3	4
List B:				

Multiply by 4 then add 7.

◆ Investigate

Finding the 'list changing' rule

a Examine the 'next term' rules above. How is each related to the 'list changing' rule?

b Find the 'list changing' rule for this table and use it to find the missing terms.

List A:	1	2	3	4	5	...	23	...	76
List B:	11	17	23	29	35	...		...	

Challenge

Paving the way

Pavlo decided to slab his path with 1 m × 2 m slabs:

He was not sure of the best pattern.
He decided to find all the possibilities for various lengths of path.

1 metre path   2 metre path   3 metre path

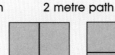 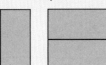 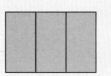 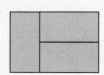

1 possibility   2 possibilities   3 possibilities

   a Continue this investigation.
      How many possible patterns are there for a 4-metre path, 5-metre path, etc?
   b What is the 'next term' rule for this sequence?
   c Have you seen this sequence before?

4   Letters and Sequences

We can use letters to describe the 'list changing' rules.

Example

List changing rule: Add 7 to A to get B						
List A:	1	2	3	4		x
List B:	8	9	10	11		x + 7

1 becomes 1 + 7 = 8
2 becomes 2 + 7 = 9
3 becomes 3 + 7 = 10
4 becomes 4 + 7 = 11

The 'list changing' rule is **x becomes x + 7**

 A

1. Using the rule 'x becomes x + 3' what do these become?
    a 2 **b** 5 **c** 12 **d** 16 **e** 32

2. Using the rule 'y becomes 4y' what do these become?
    a 3 **b** 8 **c** 10 **d** 23 **e** 40

3. Using the rule 'm becomes m – 7' what do these become?
    a 8 **b** 9 **c** 29 **d** 34 **e** 78

4. Copy and complete these tables using the given 'list changing' rule:

a x becomes $x + 1$

x	1	2	3	4	5
x + 1					

b n becomes $n - 3$

n	4	5	6	7	8
n – 3					

c w becomes $w + 8$

w	1	2	3	4	5
w + 8					

d m becomes $4m$

m	1	2	3	4	5
4m					

e h becomes $6h$

h	1	2	3	4	5
6h					

f y becomes $y - 9$

y	15	16	17	18	19
y – 9					

5. Copy and complete these tables:

a

x	1	2	3	4	5			32
x + 9								

b

w	1	2	3	4	5			23
3w								

c

r	1	2	3	4	5			32
r + 2								

d

t	1	2	3	4	5			23
10t								

Challenge

Number Grid

Complete these grids:

a

m – 5	1		15		
m		12			
5m				40	55

b

7n	35			63	84
n					
n – 4		6	3		

c

11x	22			99	
x		13			
x + 11			19		51

5 Using Letters and Sequences

Example 1 How many holes in a 17 cm bracket?

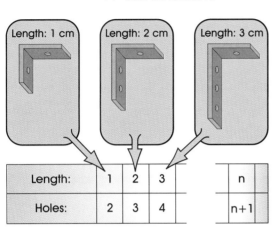

Length:	1	2	3		n
Holes:	2	3	4		n+1

Example 2 How many teeth on 21 cogwheels?

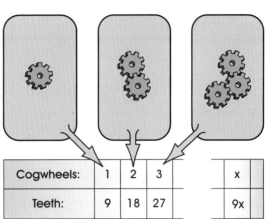

Cogwheels:	1	2	3		x
Teeth:	9	18	27		9x

1. The **rule** is 'add 1 to the number of centimetres to get the number of holes' ... **n** becomes **n + 1**.
    A 17 cm bracket would have 17 + 1 = 18 holes.

2. The rule is 'multiply the number of cogwheels by 9 to get the number of teeth' ... **x** becomes **9x**.
    21 cogwheels would have 21 × 9 = 189 teeth.

For each situation, first copy and complete the table and then answer the question.

1. How many petals are there for 18 flowers?

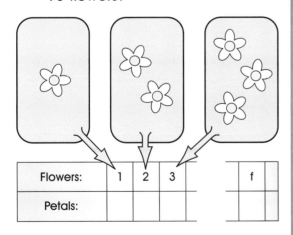

Flowers:	1	2	3		f
Petals:					

2. How many matches are there in picture 25?

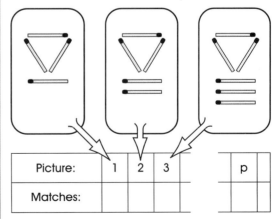

Picture:	1	2	3		p
Matches:					

189

3. How many coins are there in picture 13?

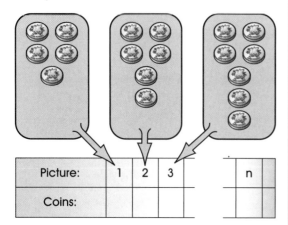

Picture:	1	2	3			n	
Coins:							

4. 35 wheels have how many spokes?

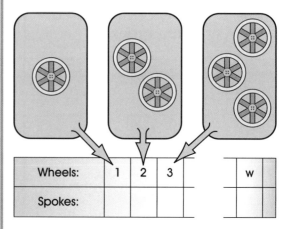

Wheels:	1	2	3			w	
Spokes:							

5. How many mushrooms would there be after one day?

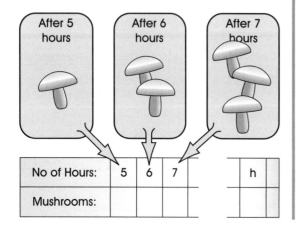

No of Hours:	5	6	7			h	
Mushrooms:							

6. How many beads are required to make up an order of 25 necklaces?

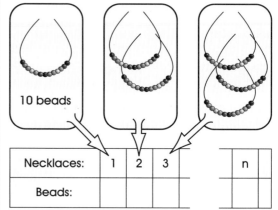

Necklaces:	1	2	3			n	
Beads:							

Challenge

Matchstick Challenge

Here are some matchstick patterns.

a 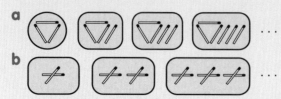 . . .

b . . .

1. Can you find the rule for the number of matches in pattern m for each pattern?

2. Create your own sequence of matchstick pattern.
Test your neighbour's ability to spot the rule.

Unit 24 Information Handling

Computers can store whole libraries of information

Databases can store vast amounts of data

Spreadsheets can be used to organise, calculate and display data

The <u>Internet</u> can be used to find data on almost every subject around the world

1 Looking Back

The information below shows **one record** from a **database** about books.

1. **a** How many *fields* make up a *record* in the book database?
   b Draw a table with seven rows and complete the first row with details of *James and the Giant Peach*.

Name of book	James and the Giant Peach
Author	Roald Dahl
Publisher	Puffin
Number of pages	156
Date of first publication	1961

Name of book	Author	Publisher	Number of pages	Date of 1st publication

c Use the information below to add the details of these three books to your table.

THE ONE MINUTE DREAM

By Colin Pearce

First Published 1990 by Armada Books Contains 155 pages

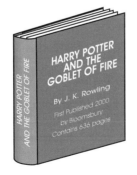

HARRY POTTER AND THE GOBLET OF FIRE

By J. K. Rowling

First Published 2000 by Bloomsbury Contains 636 pages

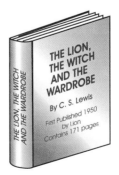

THE LION, THE WITCH AND THE WARDROBE

By C. S. Lewis

First Published 1950 by Lion Contains 171 pages

d Choose another three novels and add them to your books list.
e Which book has the most pages?
f If you have access to a computer, create a **Books Database**. Add records about the books in your list.

191

2. This table is a form used to collect information for a database called 'Class Mates'.

First Name	Surname	Date of Birth	Age (years/months)

a What are the fields in the database?

b Draw a table with lines for 5 records. Use data about yourself for the first record. Collect data about four classmates.

c Who is the oldest in your list?

d If you have access to a computer, create a **Classmates Database**. Enter the data you have collected.

3. This is information from a **Dinosaur Database**.

Name: Tyrannosaurus **Diet:** Carnivore **Name Means:** 'Tyrant Lizard' **Length (m):** 13 **Height (m):** 5	**Name:** Allosaurus **Diet:** Carnivore **Name Means:** 'Different Lizard' **Length (m):** 10 **Height (m):** 4	**Name:** Diplodocus **Diet:** Herbivore **Name Means:** 'Double Beam' **Length (m):** 27 **Height (m):** 7
Name: Plateosaurus **Diet:** Herbivore **Name Means:** 'Flat Lizard' **Length (m):** 8 **Height (m):** 3	**Name:** Triceratops **Diet:** Herbivore **Name Means:** 'Three Horn Face' **Length (m):** 9 **Height (m):** 2.7	**Name:** Velociraptor **Diet:** Carnivore **Name Means:** 'Swift Robber' **Length (m):** 3 **Height (m):** 7

a How many records are shown?

b How many fields are there making up this database?

c What are the field names?

d Which of the dinosaurs were carnivores?

e Which of the dinosaurs were shorter than 12.5 m in length?

f Name the shortest dinosaur listed.

g How many of the dinosaurs listed have names that mean a type of lizard?

4. The Primary 7 enterprise group used this table to record the takings at their fête.

	A	B	C	D	E	F
1		Baking	Books	Toys	Face Painting	Total
2	Morning	£1.50	£2.30	£1.85		
3	Afternoon			£2.35		
4	Total					

a Make a copy of this spreadsheet as a table in your jotter.

b The baking stall raised twice as much in the afternoon as the morning. Complete cell B3.

c   The book stall made the same amount in the afternoon as the baking stall. Complete cell C3.

d   Face painting cost 10p. 18 children had their faces painted in the morning and 22 in the afternoon. Complete cells E2 and E3.

e   Which cells would be added to find the total raised at the baking stall in cell B4?

f   Which cells would be added to find the total raised in the afternoon in cell F3?

g   Complete the totals in column F and row 4.

2 Creating and Using a Database

In a database there are different types of fields, each handled differently by the computer. For example:

TEXT, NUMBER, DATE, TIME, CALCULATION, SUMMARY and others.

A text field contains any string of characters.

Examples: First name (James), Phone number (0124 561789)

A number field contains single numbers that can be used in calculations.

Examples: Height (m) (2.7). The units go with the field name.

A date field contains the month, day and year in a particular format.

A time field contains clock times.

1.   There are two field types used in the Dinosaurs Database on page 192 – *text* and *number*.

What type of field is:

a   the **Name** field?   b   the **Diet** field?

c   the **Name Means** field?

d   the **Length (m)** field?   e   the **Height (m)** field?

f   In the record for the Tyrannosaurus, the field Length (m) has a value of 13. What does this mean?

2. **a** Here the database has been sorted. What field has been used to sort it? Which dinosaur will be last on the list?

Name	Diet	Name Means	Length (m)	height (m)
Allosaurus	carnivore	different lizard	10	4
Diplodocus	herbivore	double beam	27	7
Plateosaurus	herbivore	flat lizard	8	3
Ste~	herbivore	roofe~ ~	9	

b Sort the list out by height (m), tallest first. If two dinosaurs have the same height, then sort alphabetically.

c Here a search has been made for the dinosaurs that are 9 m long.

Name	Diet	Name Means	Length (m)	height (m)
Triceratops	herbivore	three horned face	9	2.7

Make out a list of the dinosaurs that are less than 10 m tall.

d If you have access to a computer, create a database about dinosaurs.

Challenge

Search in books or on the Internet for information about dinosaurs and add more records to your dinosaur database.

3. The *Countries resource sheet* contains lots of data about different countries around the world.
Select data to create a countries database, which has:

❖ three fields
❖ more than one field type
❖ at least five records.

a **Sort** your records by country name in alphabetical order. Which country is last?

b Write two search questions for others to try on your database.

3 Creating and Using a Spreadsheet

A computer spreadsheet is a program that displays data in a table with **cells** arranged in **rows** and **columns**.

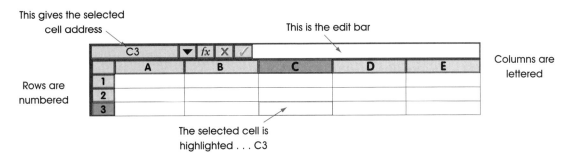

This gives the selected cell address

This is the edit bar

Columns are lettered

Rows are numbered

The selected cell is highlighted . . . C3

If we type 'SCOTLAND'

... and press **Return**	... SCOTLAND is entered in C3 and the cell below it, C4, becomes highlighted.
... or press **Tab**	... SCOTLAND is entered in C3 and the cell to the right, D3, becomes highlighted.
... or click ✔	... SCOTLAND is entered in C3 and the cell C3 remains highlighted.

Pressing ✗ deletes the entry in the selected cell.

You can enter data as:

1. a label ... any string of characters, e.g. Peter123@aol.com
2. a number ... for use in a calculation (no letters, spaces or units allowed)
3. a formula ... instructions on what to do with the numbers to be found in named cells

Example

	A	B	C	D	E	F
1		Adam	Beth	Carol	Dave	total
2	Height (m)	1.7	1.4	1.2	1.3	5.6

B1 contains the label 'Adam'
B2 contains the number 1.7

F2 contains the formula '= B2 + C2 + D2 + E2'
   ... the spreadsheet works it out and displays '5.6' in the cell.

A formula always starts with '=', so that the spreadsheet can recognise it as a formula.

A

1. Which cell is active after entering these instructions?

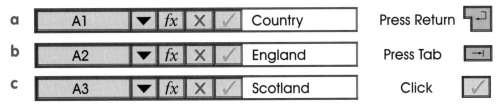

a | A1 | ▼ | fx | X | ✓ | Country | Press Return
b | A2 | ▼ | fx | X | ✓ | England | Press Tab
c | A3 | ▼ | fx | X | ✓ | Scotland | Click

2. **a** **B1** is made active. The heading **Capital** is entered and return is pressed. Which cell is now selected?

b The entry **London** is made in **B2**. You want to put **Edinburgh** into **B3**. Should you press Return or Tab?

c If you have access to a computer, enter this data in a spreadsheet.

d The table is sorted alphabetically by country. Which country will appear in A3?

e Which capital will appear in B5?

f The table is sorted alphabetically by capital. Does any country still occupy:

   i its original position?

   ii the position it held after the sort by country?

	A	B
1	Country	Capital
2	England	London
3	Scotland	Edinburgh
4	France	Paris
5	Spain	Madrid
6	Italy	Rome
7	Germany	Berlin

If you are doing this on a computer then all the cells in A2 to B7 must be selected or you may lose the connection between country and capital.

	A	B
1	Country	Capital
2	Germany	Berlin
3	Scotland	Edinburgh
4	England	London
5	Spain	Madrid
6	France	Paris
7	Italy	Rome

Challenge

Create a spreadsheet about your class's favourite subjects

1. Open a **New Spreadsheet** file.
2. Enter the headings and subject names, as shown on this spreadsheet.
3. Collect data to help you complete column B (up to cell B10) of the spreadsheet.
4. Use your spreadsheet data to help you answer these questions:

  a What is the most popular subject?

  b What is your favourite subject?

  c Is I.C.T. more popular than Art?

  d Is Maths more popular than P.E.?

  e What is the least popular subject?

  f What is in Cell B8?

  g What is in Cell A9?

  h Which Cell is the word Art in?

  i Which subjects did less than five people choose?

	A	B
1	Subject	No. of Pupils
2	Maths	
3	Language	
4	Art	
5	P.E.	
6	R.E.	
7	I.C.T.	
8	Env. Studies	
9	Drama	
10	Music	
11	Total	

Using Formulae

Numbers in cells can be used in calculations by using formulae.

Example 1	$= A1 + A2 + A3$	... this will add the numbers in the cells and put the answer in B1
Example 2	$= A1 - A2$	... this will subtract the number in A2 from that in A1 and put the answer in B1
Example 3	$= A1 * A2$	... this will multiply the numbers in the two cells and put the answer in B1
Example 4	$= A1 * 5$	... this will multiply the number in A1 by 5 and put the answer in B1
Example 5	$= A1 / 2$	... this will divide the number in A1 by 2 and put the answer in B1

	A	B	C
1	24	$= A1 + A2$	$= A1 - A2$
2	3	$= A1 * A2$	$= A1 / A2$

	A	B	C
1	24	27	21
2	3	72	8

type this ⟶ get this

B

1. Look at the forumulae in this spreadsheet.

	A	B	C
1	12	$= A1 + A2$	$= A1 - A2$
2	4	$= A1 * A2$	$= A1 / A2$
3	7	$= A1 + A2 + A3$	$= A2 * A2$
4		$= A1 + A2 - A3$	$= (A3 * A3) - (A1 * A2)$

   a What number will appear in cell:
      i B1   ii B2   iii B3?
   b Which is bigger, the answer in B3 or the answer in C3?
   c Calculate the numbers that will appear in the C column.

2. The infants at Poppleburn Primary School are going to the pantomime. Tickets cost £3 each.
   Cell C2 holds the formula $= 3 * B2$
   Cell C3 holds the formula $= 3 * B3$
   Cell C4 holds the formula $= 3 * B4$

	A	B	C	D
1	Class	No. of pupils	Ticket cost	Ice cream cost
2	1	30		
3	2	25		
4	3	29		
5	4	31		
6	Totals			

   a What is the formula in C5?
   b Cell C2 shows the number **90. (30 pupils at £3 = £90)**
      What will show in cell:
      i C3   ii C4   iii C5?

Unit 24

c B6 holds the formula = **B2 + B3 + B4 + B5** ... (the total number of pupils).
A similar formula is in C6 to calculate the total cost.

 i What is the formula?   ii What number appears in B6?

 iii What number appears in C6?

d Ice creams cost 80p.

 i What formula should be put in D2 to calculate the cost of ice creams for class 1?

 ii What value will appear in the cell?

 iii Repeat the two steps above for cells D3, D4 and D5.

Challenge

The school funds have £400. Is this enough to pay for the outing?

3. This spreadsheet shows the total cost of items bought for the classroom. Notice 6 pencils cost a total of 72p.

	A	B	C	D
1	Items	total cost (p)	no of items	cost of one (p)
2	pencil	72	6	
3	ruler	75	5	
4	rubber	56	7	
5	Totals			

 a How many rulers were bought?

 b What was the total cost of the rulers?

 c To calculate the cost of one item we divide the total cost by the number of items. In D2 we put the formula = **B2/C2**. What number will appear?

 d Write down a similar formula for D3 and D4.

 e Write down a formula for B5 (the total of money spent)

 f Write down a formula for C5 (the total number of items bought).

If you have access to a computer, try to make these spreadsheets.

4 Make Charts – Using Spreadsheets

You can make different kinds of graphs of computer spreadsheet data. Most spreadsheets will allow you to turn data into graphs and charts. Different packages use different methods.

A

1. **a** Create a spreadsheet showing the number of days in each month of a normal year.
   b Use your computer package to make a bar graph of the data.
   c Can you see why it is better to use three-letter month names?
   d Can you tell from your graph how many months have 31 days?
   e Can you tell the shortest month?

	A	B
1	Month	No. of days
2	Jan	31
3	Feb	28
4	Mar	31
5	Apr	30
6	May	31
7	Jun	30
8	Jul	31
9	Aug	31
10	Sep	
13		31

30 days hath September, all the rest I can't remember

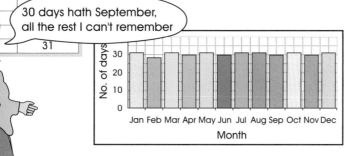

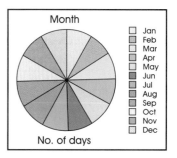

   f Use your package to make a pie chart of the data.
   g Can you tell from your graph how many months have 31 days?
   h Can you tell the shortest month?
   i Was the bar graph or pie chart more suitable for displaying this data?

2. James kept a record of noon temperatures for a week.

	A	B	C	D	E	F	G	H
1	Day	Mon	Tue	Wed	Thu	Fri	Sat	Sun
2	Temp (°C)	18	20	21	23	20	18	18

   a Enter the data in your spreadsheet.
   b Use it to make a bar chart, a line graph and a pie chart.
   c Which chart is most suitable, and which is not suitable?
   d Which chart is best for showing the trend in noon temperatures?

3. Jenny did a survey of how many siblings (brothers or sisters) each pupil in her class had.

	A	B	C	D	E	F	G
1	No. of siblings	None	One	Two	Three	Four	Five
2	Frequency	3	5	4	3	1	1

   a   Make your own spreadsheet of this data.

   b   Use the data to help you create a bar chart, a line graph and a pie chart.

   c   Which is most suitable for this sort of data? Why?

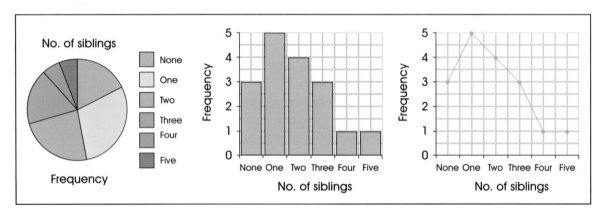

4. Jamilah bought a bag of toffees and examined the contents:
12 liquorice, 7 dairy, 9 mint, 14 strawberry, 14 banana.

   a   Make a spreadsheet to hold the data.

   b   Make a pie chart to display the data.
Remember to give a title and provide a *legend* (key).
Use your chart to answer the following:

   c   Which flavour is represented by the smallest sector?

   d   Which two flavours together make up half the chart?

Unit 25 Decimals

1 Looking Back

1. Here is a number line. The small un-numbered marks represent tenths (0·1).

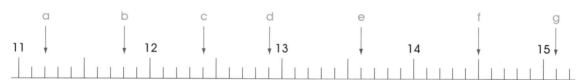

Write in decimal form the number that each of the arrows point to.

2. Here is another number line. The small un-numbered marks represent hundredths (0·01).

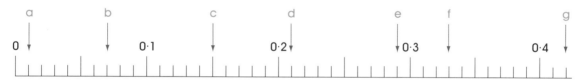

Write in decimal form the number that each of the arrows point to.

3. Write the value of each blue digit in the following numbers:

a 234·7   b 17·6   c 13·97   d 11·02   e 98·01   f 700·5

4. Write the following in words:

a 9·3 b 87·7 c 11·65 d 200·4 e 90·06 f 270·09

5. Write these as numbers:

   a Twelve point six
   b thirty seven point one seven
   c six point zero nine
   d one hundred point two five

6. Write out each list in order, smallest first.

   a 12·7   10·8   0·6   12·1   8·5   9·0
   b 16·6 kg   20·2 kg   5·9 kg   33·3 kg   40·8 kg   19·9 kg
   c 35·45 m   11·70 m   98·29 m 70·40 m   8·23 m   70·04 m
   d £23·35   £57·70   £11   £57·07   £10·20   £0·79

7. What is the reading on each scale?

8. The labels show the heights of the trees. Match each label with a tree.

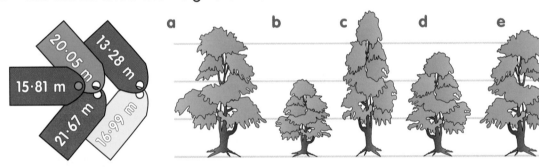

9. Alistair and Hannah turned over four digit
   cards each.
   They use their numbers to play a game.

   Alistair's number

   Using all of their digits and a decimal point,
   they must make the *largest number* they can
   with a digit in the first decimal place.

   Hannah's number

   a Alistair makes 853·1
      Can Hannah make a larger number and
      win?

   b In the next round they have to make the
      smallest number with two decimal places.
      Who will be the winner this time?

Challenge

Elaine picked four different digit cards and made a number to two decimal places.

❖ The tenths digit is the smallest possible odd number.
❖ The tens digit is the largest possible odd number.
❖ The units digit is four times larger than the hundredths digit.

What is Elaine's number?

2 Round, Round, Round

A

1. Round each of the following to the nearest whole number:

   a 8·8   b 13·2   c 67·5   d 27·4   e 277·7   f 420·5
   g 199·7   h 4·39   i 18·78   j 48·87   k 21·50   l 88·22

2. Round the length of each vehicle to the nearest metre.

   a

   14·45 m

   b

   16·49 m

   c
   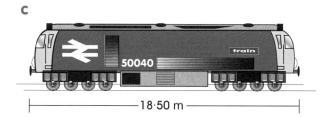
   18·50 m

   d

   3.81 m

3. Round the following to the nearest 10 and then to the nearest 100.

   a 124·7   b 567·2   c 325·8 kg   d 259·7 km   e £75·30

4. Round these numbers to the nearest whole number and **estimate** the answer to the calculation:

   a 5·6 + 2·6   b 11·5 + 5·3   c 10·9 − 8·1   d 13·5 + 7·8
   e 20·2 − 13·9   f 17·4 + 12·5   g 50·28 − 29·50   h 41·51 − 6·61

5. Four friends saved up money for their school trip.
   Kyle saved **£7·89**   Lara saved **£10·50**
   Justin saved **£9·43**   Rachel saved **£9·62**

   a Which two children saved **about** £20 between them?
   b Which three children saved **about** £29 in total?

Challenge

Mr and Mrs Templeton went to the supermarket for their weekly shopping.

They packed their shopping into five bags weighing:

Mr Templeton carried two bags with a total weight of **about** 19 kg.
Mrs Templeton carried three bags with a total weight of **about** 20 kg

Which bags did each carry?

4·6 kg   9·3 kg   7·8 kg   6·2 kg   10·5 kg

---

3 Multiplying and Dividing by 10 and 100

A

1. Work out the following:

   a 4·6 × 10   b 0·46 × 10   c 22·57 × 10 d 18·06 × 10 e 0·07 × 10
   f 432·1 × 10 g 19·8 × 100 h 2·56 × 100 i 0·35 × 100 j 30·7 × 100

2. The volume of one carton of Vitajuice is 1·75 litres.
   Calculate:

   a the volume of 10 cartons   b the volume of 100 cartons.

3. Turn each measurement into millimetres [by multiplying by 10].

   a 2·3 cm   b 33·25 cm   c 100·9 cm   d 62 cm

4. Turn each amount into pennies [by multiplying by 100].

   a £2·99   b £9·08   c £12·50   d £36·00

5. Calculate:

   a 7·0 ÷ 10   b 29·0 ÷ 10   c 321 ÷ 10   d 5·7 ÷ 10   e 30·4 ÷ 10
   f 7 ÷ 100   g 45 ÷ 100   h 71·3 ÷ 100 i 109 ÷ 100   j 470 ÷ 100

6. The cost of ten football coaching lessons is £120. What is the cost of one lesson?

7. Turn the following into centimetres [divide by 10].

   a 9·4 mm   b 748 mm   c 1·9 mm
   d 10·3 mm   e 201·7 mm   f 6 mm

8. Turn each amount into pounds [divide by 100].

   a 287p   b 945p   c 1252p
   d 4p   e 57p   f 103p

◆ Investigate

Here is a magic square with each side, column and diagonal adding up to 15.

a If we divide each number by 10, is it still a magic square?
b What happen if we divide each number by 100?

4	9	2
3	5	7
8	1	6

 Decimal Calculations

1. Work out the following:

a 23·5	b 83·8	c 283·5	d 49·26	e 47·28	f 41·08
+ 15·6	+ 7·5	+ 29·7	+ 22·57	+ 52·71	+ 29·99

g 56·5	h 60·8	i 405·3	j 88·32	k 70·06	l 90·00
− 22·7	− 37·5	− 26·9	− 25·15	− 23·22	− 37·11

2. Calculate:

   a 55·7 + 12·9   b 42·16 − 11·85   c 57·82 + 8·68
   d 70 − 11·35   e 43·02 + 33·99

3. Jason took two bags on a week-long holiday.
   One bag weighed 8·8 kg, the other 13·7 kg.

   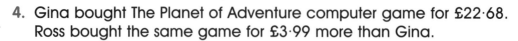

   a What was the total weight of the two bags?
   b Debbie took one suitcase weighing 25 kg.
     Calculate the difference in the weight of Jason's
     and Debbie's luggage.

4. Gina bought The Planet of Adventure computer game for £22·68.
   Ross bought the same game for £3·99 more than Gina.

   a How much did Ross pay for his computer game?
   b If Gina paid for her game with a £50 note, how much change did she
     get?
   c Ross paid the exact amount of money using the fewest possible coins.
     Write down the notes and coins with which he paid.

5. Calculate:

a	3·7	b	18·8	c	17·7	d	13·57	e	8·63
	× 3		× 4		× 6		× 5		× 9

   f 3⟌42·3   g 6⟌307·2   h 6⟌486·6   i 5⟌76·30

6. Work out the following:

   a 13·7 × 6   b 14·4 ÷ 6   c 8·73 × 9   d 34·88 ÷ 8   e 7·68 × 9

7. On one day in January, the temperature for Perth **in Australia** was 29·6°C.
   This was eight times the temperature for Perth **in Scotland**.
   What was the temperature for Perth in Scotland?

8. One lap round a local park is 2·48 km. Ben cycled four laps round the
   park. Gemma cycled three laps more that Ben.

   a What distance did each child cycle?
   b How much further did Gemma cycle?

9. Mrs Curry paid £89·94 for a new microwave oven. She paid in six equal
   instalments.
   How much is each instalment?

10. A special six pack of Coola Cola contains 6 × 2·75 litre
    bottles.
    a What is the total volume of cola in the pack?
    b Round your answer to the nearest litre.
    c Tanya bought three of the special packs for a party
      and paid with £30.
      She was given £6·78 change in coins only.
      List the coins in her change if she was given the
      fewest possible coins.

Challenge

Use the information above to work out the cost of **1 bottle** of Coola Cola.

Remember to line up the decimal points ...

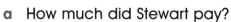

B

1. Calculate:

a 36·7 + 29·9	b 71·2 − 26·7	c 136·7 + 54·8
d 123·7 − 30·9	e 120·2 − 26·4	f 64·33 + 39·78
g 60·27 − 19·65	h 59·97 + 30·47	i 68·08 + 29·92

2. At a Royal garden party there were two swan ice sculptures each weighing 38·6 kg and 55·7 kg.

   a Calculate the combined weight of the two sculptures.
   b What was the difference in the weight of the two sculptures?

3. Mr Goodhew was looking in a catalogue at two garden swimming pools. The Mega pool held 170·3 litres of water and the Superfun pool held 138·8 litres.
   How many more litres of water did the Mega pool hold?

4. John bought a new guitar for £53·75. His friend Stewart bought the same guitar in a different shop for £8·99 more.

   a How much did Stewart pay?
   b List the smallest amount of notes and coins Stewart needed to pay for his guitar.

   John paid for his guitar with three twenty pound notes.
   c What change did he get back?
   d List the notes and coins in his change if he was given the smallest number possible.

5. Work out:

a 76·4 × 6	b 58·8 ÷ 4	c 127·5 × 7	d 142·2 ÷ 6
e 37·25 × 8	f 51·45 ÷ 5	g 129·7 × 7	h 80·46 ÷ 9
i 72·48 ÷ 8	j 16·66 × 6	k 90·54 ÷ 9	

6. The distance of the London Marathon is 41·92 km.
Amanda completed $\frac{1}{4}$ of it in an hour

   a How far had she run?
   b How far did she still have to run?

7. A delivery van can safely hold 916 kg.
How many 114·5 kg crates could be put in
the van?

8. Greg bought some new T-shirts for £12·87 each.
He spent £90·09 in total.
How many T-shirts did he buy?

Challenge

Which two numbers?

The sum of these two numbers
is 91·25.

Their difference is 3·89.

47·47 48·66 42·59 43·68 43·58 47·57

---

5 Calculator Work

1. Calculate the difference in the total
weight between:

   a yellow and red presents
   b purple and red presents
   c yellow and purple presents

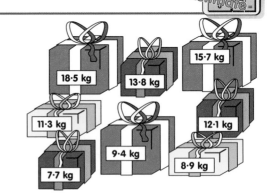

2. Work these out:

   a $(12·8 \times 7) \div 4$ **b** $(84·6 \div 9) \times 3$
   c $(11·55 \times 8) \div 6$ **d** $(92·28 \div 6) \times 5$

3. The Royal Cinema sells popcorn in three different-sized buckets:

    Find the cost of:
    a   27 Mega buckets   b   39 Large buckets
    c   45 Regular buckets   d   23 Large and 17 Regular
        buckets
    e   A school party of 33 children each bought the same size of popcorn
        bucket. They spent £94·05 in total.
        What size of bucket did they all buy?

    Regular £1·99
    Large £2·49
    Mega £2·85

4. In a roller-blading race, competitors travelled round a special track 50 times.
    They covered a total distance of 37·5 km.
    What is the distance round one lap of the track?

Challenge

Select four numbers that when added together make the Star Total in the middle.

? — 13·8
45·2   9·4   41·7
100   15·9
? — ?   34·9   6·1
13·8

? — ?
12·15
11·09   11·39
50   14·07
? — ?   14·24   13·76
13·28

B

1. Calculate:

    a   33·7 litres + 43·8 litres + 60·4 litres   b   450·1 kg − 236·6 kg
    c   29·75 km + 19·28 km + 43·21 km   d   50·2 + 73·9 − 62·8
    e   80·12 − 27·38 + 41·72   f   21·67 + 73·09 − 53·75

2. Work out the difference between the perimeters of:

    a   the flower bed and the whole garden
    b   the vegetable patch and the flower bed
    c   the vegetable patch and the whole garden.

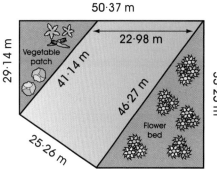

50·37 m
29·14 m
Vegetable patch
22·98 m
41·14 m
46·27 m
35·25 m
Flower bed
25·26 m
31·28 m

3. To visit his family, Hamish had to travel 136·7 km by train, 31·9 km by bus and 5·7 km by taxi.

    a What was the total distance of his journey?
    b He spent £52·94 in total getting there.
       The train cost £39·99.
       How much did he spend on the bus and taxi together?
    c The taxi trip cost £3·25 more than the price of the bus ticket.
       How much did the taxi and the bus cost?

4. What number comes out of each function machine?

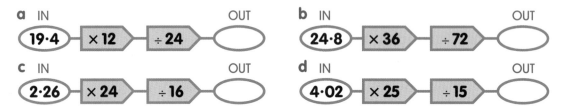

a IN   19·4   × 12   ÷ 24   OUT

b IN   24·8   × 36   ÷ 72   OUT

c IN   2·26   × 24   ÷ 16   OUT

d IN   4·02   × 25   ÷ 15   OUT

Challenge

Scott had some birthday money to spend.
He buys:
- three CDs costing £12·99 each
- a dozen new pencils for school costing 15p each
- two sports tops costing £19·99 each
- 15 packs of football stickers costing 39p.

He was left with £4·40.   How much birthday money did he start with?

Volume and Weight

Which is heavier 100 kilograms of bricks or 100 kilograms of feathers?

They both weigh the same although the pile of feathers would be much larger than the pile of bricks.

1 Looking Back

weight
pints
minutes
length
kilograms
litres
scales
volume
seconds
time
metres
ruler

1. Sort these measurement words into the four lists below.

list 1

list 3

list 3

list 4

2. Write down the volume of liquid in each jug.

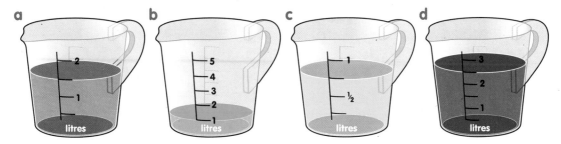

a
b
c
d

litres   litres   litres   litres

3. One full mug contains $\frac{1}{4}$ litre of liquid. One full jug contains $1\frac{1}{2}$ litres of liquid.

   a In these pictures the mugs and jars are all full.
   How much liquid is in each picture?

   How many mugs could be filled from:
   b 1 litre of water   c 2 litres of water   d 3 litres of water?
   How many jugs could be filled from:
   e 3 litres of water   f 7 litres of water   g 9 litres of water?
   h How many mugs could be filled from
   one full jug?
   i The bucket holds 10 litres of water. How
   many full jugs and extra mugs could
   be filled from the bucket?

4. Dice are piled together to form solids. Each of the dice is the same size.

   i 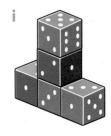   ii    iii 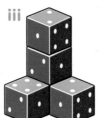   iv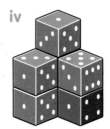

   a Which solid has the largest volume?   b Which solid has the smallest
   volume?

5. Write these weights in grams:

   a 4 kg 430g   b 8 kg 290g   c 3 kg 75g   d 4 kg 999g   e 9 kg 86g

6. Copy and complete, writing the weights in:
   ❖ kilograms and grams   ❖ grams only.

   a 2·520 kg   = 2 kg 520 g = 2520g
   b 2·040 kg   = _ kg ___ g = ___ g
   c 9·305 kg   = _ kg ___ g = ___ g
   d 6·217 kg   = _ kg ___ g = ___ g
   e 76·421 kg = _ kg ___ g = ___ g

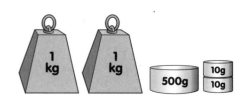

7. i Give the weight of each parcel in kilograms.
ii Express this weight in grams.

a  b  c  d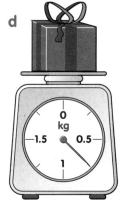

8. Read the volumes and weights being measured to the nearest mark.

a  b 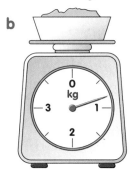 c  d

2 Volume – Litres and Millilitres

 A

> **1000 ml = 1 litre**

1. How many millilitres are there in:

a $\frac{1}{2}$ litre   b $\frac{1}{4}$ litre   c $\frac{3}{4}$ litre   d $\frac{1}{10}$ litre   e $\frac{1}{5}$ litre?

2. How many millilitres of liquid are in each container?

a  b  c  d  e

3. Write these volumes in millilitres:

   a 3 litres   **b** 15 litres   **c** 29 litres   **d** 50 litres
   e $2\frac{1}{2}$ litres   **f** $7\frac{1}{4}$ litres   **g** $22\frac{3}{4}$ litres   **h** $40\frac{1}{10}$ litres

4. Write these volumes using millilitres only:

   a 6 litres 250 ml   **b** 1 litre 476 ml   **c** 12 litres 236 ml
   d 9 litres 505 ml   **e** 10 litre 22 ml

5. Change these measurements from litres to millilitres:

   a 2·234 litres   **b** 3·1 litres   **c** 42·6 litres   **d** 0·150 litres   **e** 0·03 litres

6. Write each volume in litres:

   a 4000 ml   **b** 2000 ml   **c** 19 000 ml   **d** 20 000 ml   **e** 1000 ml

7. Write these volumes in litres and millilitres:

   a 3200 ml   **b** 7650 ml   **c** 12 800 ml   **d** 14 765 ml   **e** 21 050 ml

8. Write these volumes in litres only:

   a 5210 ml   **b** 7589 ml   **c** 3218 ml   **d** 19 203 ml   **e** 53 020 ml

9. **a** List the items in order of volume, smallest to largest.
   b Which items contain more than $\frac{1}{2}$ litre?
   c Which items contain less than 350 ml?

Coola Cola   **Fabric Softener**   **Milk**

Honey   **Orange Juice**

B

1. The supermarket was running a special offer on Washing-up Liquid.

    a What is the volume of one bottle of 'Apple Bubbles'?
    b How many litres could you buy for £1·50?
    c How many millilitres of 'Apple Bubbles' could you buy for £3?

    Offer of the week
    Apple Bubbles
    Litre bottle now larger
    with an extra 250 ml free
    Still only 75p per bottle

2. The fish tank has a crack in it. It is not leaking yet, but Lisa is worried about the poor fish!
    The fish tank holds 30 litres of water.
    Lisa uses two buckets (one for each fish). She splits the water from the fish tank equally between the buckets.

    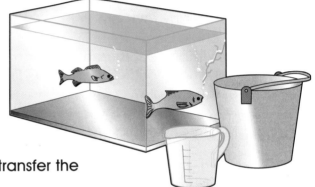

    a What volume of water will be in each bucket?
    b She uses a 750 ml jug to transfer the water.
       How many jugfuls will it take to transfer the water?

Challenge

Miss Rashid is buying diluting juice to give each of the 33 pupils in her class a drink.

One litre of 'Juicy Thirst' can be diluted to give eight drinks.

2 litres

Dilute
Orange
750 ml

a How many bottles of 'Juicy Thirst' would Miss Rashid need to buy?
b What volume of 'Juicy Thirst' would be left in the last bottle?
c How many extra drinks could be made from this?

Each glass of juice is diluted with 1/4 litre of water.

d What would be the volume of one full glass of diluted juice?
e How many jugs of water would be needed to dilute the pupils' juice?

3 Volume of Cuboids

Each edge of this cube is 1 cm long.
The volume of the cube is 1 cubic centimetre (1 cm³).

1000 cm³ = 1 litre

1 cm³ is $\frac{1}{1000}$ of a litre = 1 millilitre

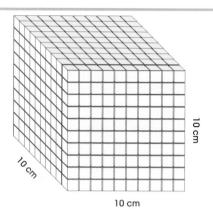

10 cm
10 cm
10 cm

A

1. a How many rows are in the bottom layer of cubic centimetres?
   b How many cubic centimetres make a row?
   c How many cubic centimetres fill the bottom layer of the cuboid?
   d How many such layers would fill the cuboid?
   e How many cubic centimetres are needed to fill the box?

3 cm
3 cm
6 cm

2. Repeat the steps in question 1 above to find how many cubic centimetres are needed to fill each of the following cuboids.

   a

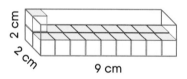

   2 cm
   2 cm
   9 cm

   b

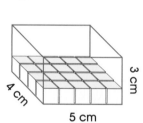

   4 cm
   3 cm
   5 cm

   c

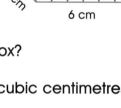

   5 cm
   3 cm
   3 cm

   d

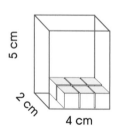

   5 cm
   2 cm
   4 cm

   e

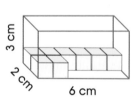

   3 cm
   2 cm
   6 cm

> **Volume = number of cm³ in a row × number of rows × number of layers.**
>
> **= length (cm) × breadth (cm) × height (cm)**
>
> **V = L × B × H**

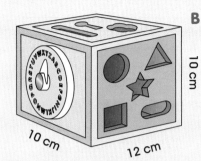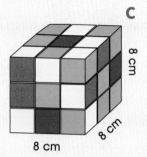

Challenge

The edges of the cuboids are measured in centimetres.

a Copy and complete the table to help you find the volume of each.

A

B

C

length × breadth × height = Volume of a cuboid

Cuboid	Length in cm	Breadth in cm	Height in cm	Volume in cm
A				
B				
C				

b Which cuboid has the smallest volume?

4 Weight

A

1000 g = 1 kg

1. Change these weights into grams:

a 4·367 kg   **b** 2·361 kg   **c** 9·426 kg   **d** 0·034 kg   **e** 3·04 kg

2. Change these weights into kilograms:

a 6387 grams   **b** 9002 grams   **c** 234 grams
d 54 grams   **e** 120 grams

3. Write these weights in kilograms and grams:

a 3·567 kg   **b** 2·200 kg   **c** 5·4 kg   **d** 21·021 kg
e 1·15 kg   **f** 3018 grams   **g** 7035 grams   **h** 1056 grams
i 7006 grams   **j** 524 grams

4. Tom and his mum both fill a bag with Pic'n'mix sweets.
Tom's bag weighs 356 grams. His mum's bag weighs 244 grams.

a What is the total weight of both bags in   i grams?   ii kilograms?
b 100 g of sweets cost 60p. What is the total cost of the sweets?

5. A new box of washing powder weighs 670 grams.
Sarah weighs her box, which she has already used, and finds it weighs $\frac{1}{4}$ kg.
How many grams of soap powder have been used?

6. Sort these items into the two sets in the table below.

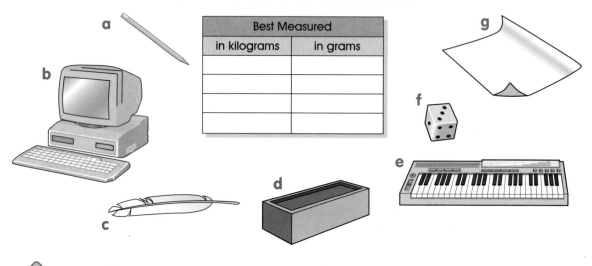

Best Measured	
in kilograms	in grams

B

1. This graph shows the weights of a
group of five pupils.

a List the weights in order
(heaviest to lightest).
b Find the difference in weight
between the heaviest and
lightest pupils.
c Find the total weight of all five
pupils.

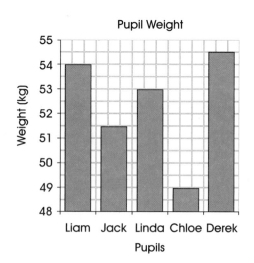

Pupil Weight

2. A spring balance is often used to weigh objects that won't fit on normal scales.

A fisherman has weighed his catch.

Fish 1   Fish 2   Fish 3   Fish 4

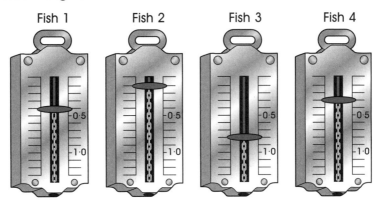

    a List the weight of each fish in:
      ❖ kilograms
      ❖ grams.
    b Find the difference in weight between the heaviest and the lightest fish.
    c The fisherman sells his fish for £3·00 per 500 grams.
      How much would he receive for this catch?

3. The pupils at Kirkland Primary School have been collecting special tokens from the supermarket to get free maths equipment for their school.
They must weigh the labels and sort them in **250 gram** bags.

List **six** different ways of using the weights shown to measure 250 grams.

(You may use each weight more than once.)

Challenge

Five calculators are given for every 0·5 kg of tokens collected.
The school collects 5 kg of tokens.
How many calculators would they be able to get with half of the tokens?

Unit 27 Two Dimensions

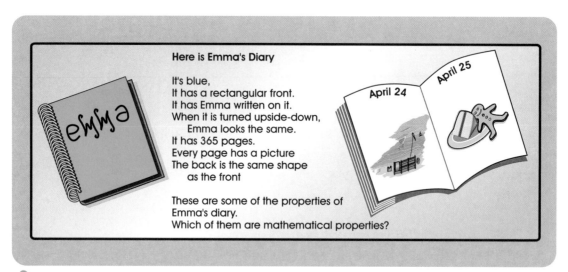

Here is Emma's Diary

It's blue,
It has a rectangular front.
It has Emma written on it.
When it is turned upside-down,
    Emma looks the same.
It has 365 pages.
Every page has a picture
The back is the same shape
    as the front

These are some of the properties of
Emma's diary.
Which of them are mathematical properties?

1 Looking Back

1. Name each of the following shapes. Describe each shape, writing about the sides and angles.

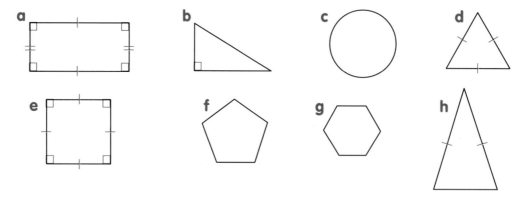

a   b   c   d

e   f   g   h

2. What is the basic difference between the seven-sided shape and the outline of the 20p piece?

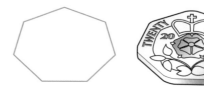

3.

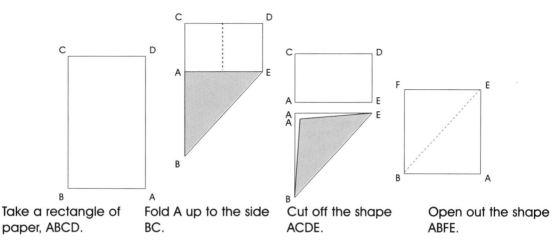

Take a rectangle of paper, ABCD.　　Fold A up to the side BC.　　Cut off the shape ACDE.　　Open out the shape ABFE.

a How can you tell that ABFE is a **square**?
b How can you tell that ACDE is a **rectangle**?

4. a A rectangle has two axes (lines) of symmetry.
Draw a rectangle and show both axes using dotted lines.
b A square has four axes of symmetry.
Draw a square and show all four axes.
c A circle has an infinite number of axes of symmetry.
Draw a circle and show one axis.
Draw a triangle with:
d one axis　　**e** three axes　　**f** no axes of symmetry.

5. a Copy and continue this tiling of a rectangle.　　**b** Copy and continue this tiling of a square.

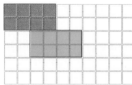　　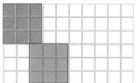

c Copy and continue this tiling of a triangle.

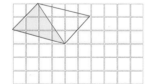

Circles don't tile. ... but we can make shapes based on circles that do.

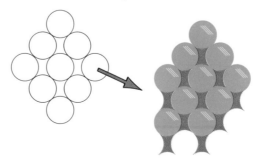

2 Naming Shapes

…tres, quattuor, quinque, sex, septem, octo, novem, decem…

An ancient Greek warrior counting from 3 to 10.

…treis, tetra, pente, hex, hepta, okto, ennea, deka…

An ancient Roman warrior counting from 3 to 10.

This is a hexagon
from the Greek words
Hex … six and
gonia … angle

… a shape with six
angles and six sides.

This is a quadrilateral
from the Latin words
quattuor … four and
latus … side

… a shape with four
angles and four sides.

A

1. Here are a collection of **penta**gons, **hexa**gons, **hepta**gons and **octo**gons.
   Copy the table and complete it to help you sort them out.
   [Counting sides might be easier.]

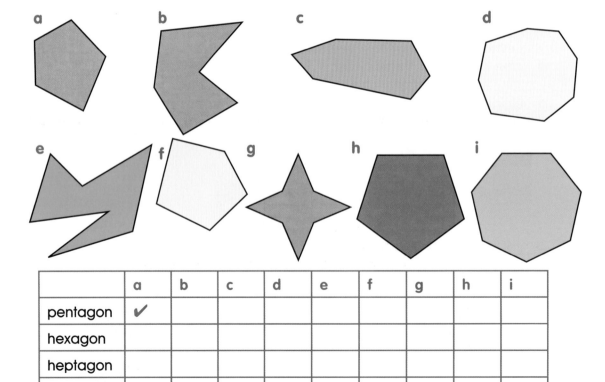

	a	b	c	d	e	f	g	h	i
pentagon	✔								
hexagon									
heptagon									
octogon									

2. In modern times the word enneagon has been replaced by nonagon.

    a Draw a nonagon.
    b How many sides has a decagon?
    c Draw a decagon.

3. The family of shapes with straight lines are called the polygons from the Greek word *polys* meaning 'much'.

    If all the sides are the same size and all the angles are the same size then the shape is said to be regular.
    Here are some regular polygons.

    Name each one:

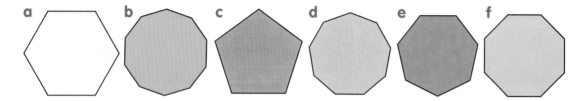

4. a The regular hexagon tiles.
       Make a sketch to show this.
    b The regular pentagon will not tile, but you can make pentagons that will. Show how each of these pentagons tile:

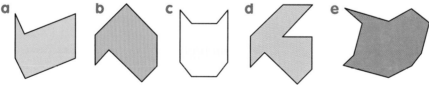

B

1. Use tracing paper to help you decide which of the following polygons tile.

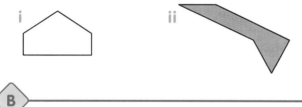

2. If the sides of a polygon of more than 4 sides are extended in both directions, a star is formed.
   The fancy term for it is 'stellated' ... here is a *stellated* pentagon.

   Draw a stellated:
       a hexagon
       b heptagon
       c octagon
       d nonagon.

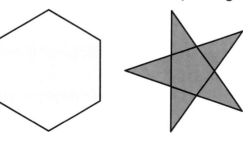

Challenge

A regular pentagon combines with a non-regular pentagon to tile.

A regular heptagon combines with a non-regular heptagon to tile.

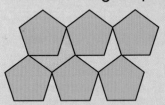

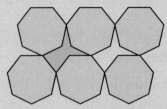

a Continue the tiling.

b Continue the tiling.

Does this work with **c** the octagon **d** the nonagon **e** the decagon?

3 ▷ Diagonals

Here are five points placed at the vertices of a regular pentagon.

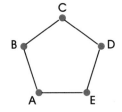 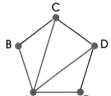 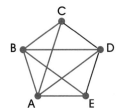 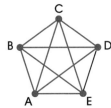 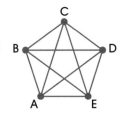

From A I can draw a red line to the other 4 points.

From B I can draw a new red line to the 3 points left.

From C I can draw a new red line to the 2 points left.

From D I can draw a new red line to the 1 point left.

For a five-sided figure I can draw 4 + 3 + 2 + 1 = 10 lines in this way.
Five of those lines are sides and so the rest must be diagonals.
The pentagon has 10 − 5 = 5 diagonals.

 A

1. **a** Copy the hexagon into your jotter and join the points as shown.
   b How many lines have you drawn?
   c How many of the lines are the sides of the hexagon?
   d How many of the lines are diagonals?
   e How many diagonals has a hexagon?

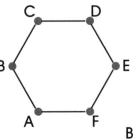

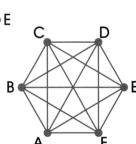

2. **a** Repeat this drawing exercise for the heptagon.
   b How many diagonals does it have?

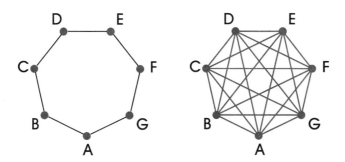

3. Without drawing, calculate the number of diagonals to be found in:

   a an octagon   **b** a nonagon   **c** a decagon.

   What does this mean?
   Three less than the number of sides **times** the number of sides **times** a half.

4. Sometimes the diagonal will go outside the shape.

   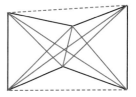

   Trace the polygons below and show their diagonals.
   Use dotted lines if the diagonal goes outside the shape.

   a 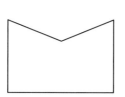   **b**   **c**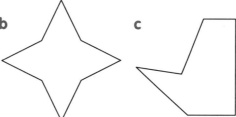

B

1. A hexagon has vertices at A(2, 3), B(0, 6), C(2, 9),
   D(6, 9), E and F.
   It has a line of symmetry passing through (4, 0) and
   (4, 10) as shown.

   a What are the coordinates of   **i** E   **ii** F?
   b What are the coordinates of the point where:
       i the diagonals CF and DA cross?
       ii the diagonals AC and BE cross?
   c Where does the line AF cut the line of symmetry?

   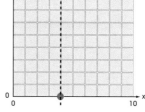

2. PQRST is a pentagon.
The table shows where the diagonals cross each other.

QT cuts PR	(4, 8)
PR cuts QS	(5, 10)
QS cuts RT	(7, 10)
RT cuts SP	(8, 8)
SP cuts QT	(6, 6)

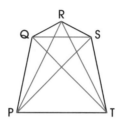

a On a suitable grid plot the points where the diagonals cross.
b Draw the diagonals to find the vertices of the pentagon.
c State the coordinates of P, Q, R, S and T.
d The shape has a line of symmetry.
Give the coordinates of the point where this line cuts the x-axis

4 Circles

A

1. a Draw a circle by drawing round a circular object.
b Lay another sheet of paper on top of the circle so that one corner just touches the circumference.
Mark points A and B where the circle disappears under the sheet.
c Joining A to B will give a diameter.
Measure the diameter of your circle.
d Turn the spare sheet of paper and, making one corner touch the circle, mark off points C and D, where the circle is disappearing under the sheet.

a

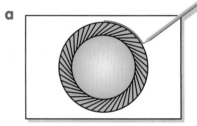

b

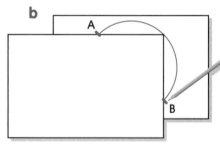

c

d

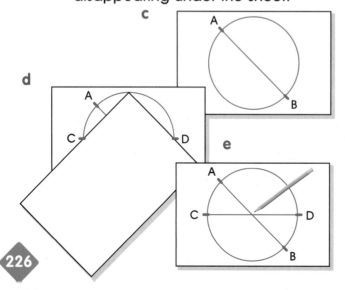

e

e Join C to D to get another diameter.
Mark the centre of the circle.
Measure the radius of the circle.
You should find that
the diameter is twice the radius.
f Check this with different circular objects.

2. What is the radius of the circle with a diameter of:

    a 10 cm   b 24 cm   c 7 m   d 12 mm?

3. What is the diameter of the circle with a radius of:

    a 6 cm   b 18 mm   c 2.5 m   d 3.25 m?

4. For each circle:

    i   measure the
        diameter
    ii calculate the
        radius.

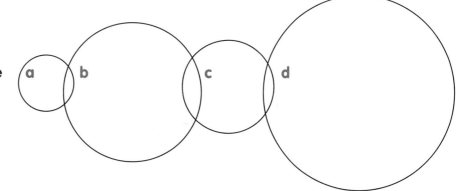

5. With the aid of a set of compasses, draw circles of diameter:

    a 8 cm   b 10 cm   c 9·6 cm

6. You can use compasses to draw an equilateral triangle.

    a Draw a 6 cm line.
    b With the compass point at one end, P, draw an arc of
       radius 6 cm.
    c With the compass point at the other end, Q, draw an arc of
       radius 6 cm.
    d Where the two arcs cross, R, marks the third vertex of the triangle.

7. Drawing regular polygons using a pair of compasses.

    a 360° ÷ 5 = 72°. Draw five lines coming away from a point, A,
       72° apart.
    b With centre A and a convenient radius, draw a circle.

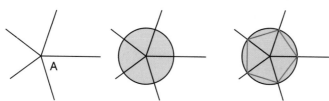

    c Join the points where the circle cuts the lines to make a pentagon.
    d 360° ÷ 6 = 60°. Draw a regular hexagon.
    e 360° ÷ 8 = 45°. Draw a regular octogon.
    f 360° ÷ 9 = 40°. Draw a regular nonagon.
    g Draw a regular decagon.
    h A duodecagon has 12 sides. Draw a regular duodecagon.

Three Dimensions

How many faces has Big Ben?

In this picture you can see 2-D shapes and 3-D shapes. Spot the squares, rectangles, triangles and circles. Spot the pyramid, cube and cuboid.

1 Looking Back

1. Name each 3-D shape below.

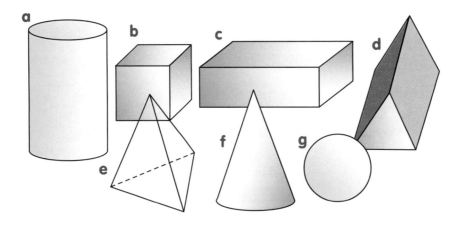

2. 2-D shapes are referred to in geometry as plane figures. They have length and breadth only (2 dimensions).
When we add thickness, we are dealing with solid shapes (3 dimensions).

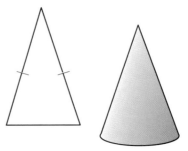

Copy and complete this table for the following
2-D and 3-D shapes.
Put a tick in the correct column.

Name of shape	2D	3D
circle	✔	
cone		
triangle		
rectangle		
cube		
cuboid		
square		
prism		
pyramid		
hexagon		
pentagon		

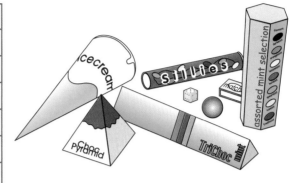

Start a class collection of 3-D shapes
you find in packaging.

2 Faces, Vertices and Edges

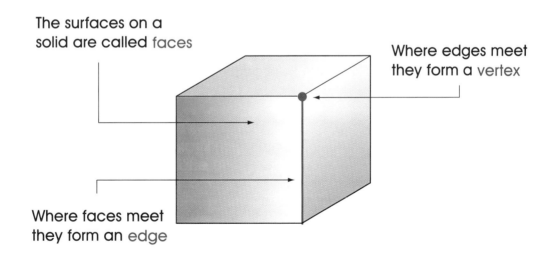

The surfaces on a
solid are called faces

Where edges meet
they form a vertex

Where faces meet
they form an edge

A

1. a Cubes are often used in packaging. Why?
   b How many faces, vertices and edges has a cube?
   c Why are dice formed from cubes?

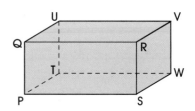

2. The cube in the picture is called ABCDEFGH. Name:

   a the tope face
   b the edges passing through A
   c the vertex where BC and CG meet.
   d What other edge meets at this vertex?

3. A building brick is in the shape of a cuboid. Why is this a good shape for a brick?

4. Here is a glass brick! It's called PQRSTUVW.

   a Name the top and bottom faces.
   b Name the front and back faces.
   c Name the left and right faces.

5. For the glass brick, name:

   a all eight vertices
   b the vertex formed where PS and SW meet
   c the three edges that meet at W.
   d How many vertices are there in a cuboid?
   e The cube and cuboid have the same number of faces, vertices and edges. How do we tell them apart? (Discuss the shape of the faces.)

6. **Prisms** are a family of shapes. Their end faces are identical shapes and the edges joining one end to the other are straight, equal and parallel. They take their name from the shape of the end face. The end face is referred to as the **base**.

| triangular prism | rectangular prism (cuboid) | pentagonal prism | hexagonal prism | heptagonal prism | circular prism (cylinder) |

Use the diagrams on the previous page to help you copy and complete the table.

Name of prism	Edges on end face	No. of faces	No. of vertices	No. of edges
triangular	3			
rectangular	4	6	8	12
pentagonal	5			
hexagonal	6			
heptagonal	7			

7. a A triangular prism has 5 faces. The triangle has 3 sides.
       A rectangular prism has 6 faces. The rectangle has 4 sides.
       Make similar statements about:
       i pentagonal prism
       ii hexagonal prism.
    b There is a rule connecting the number of faces and the number of sides.
       Can you spot it?
    c There is also a rule connecting the number of sides the base has and the number of edges and vertices.
       Find both rules.
    d Use your rules to find the number of faces, vertices and edges that an octagonal prism has.

8. The cylinder is a special prism.
    A cylinder has three faces counting the curved surface as one face.

    a What is the shape of the base?
    b How many edges has the cylinder?
    c How many vertices has it?
    d Name some examples of cylinders that you might find around the house.
    e Look at how some cylinders are stacked in supermarkets.
       Do they stack well?
    f Do cylinders fit together well? Explain your answer.

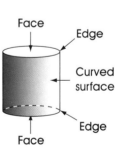

Face

Edge

Curved surface

Edge

Face

9. A solid has a 2-D base and from each vertex there rises an edge. All of these edges meet at a single point. Such a solid is called a **pyramid**. The single point is called the **apex** of the pyramid.

| triangular based pyramid | square based pyramid | pentagonal based pyramid | hexagonal based pyramid | circular based pyramid (cone) |

a Copy and complete the table.

Shape of base	No of sides on base	Faces	Vertices	Edges
triangle	3	4		
square	4		5	
pentagon	5			
hexagon	6			

b *The number of faces is one more than the number of sides on the base.*
  Make a similar connection between the number of vertices and the number of sides on the base.
c What is the connection between the number of edges and the number of sides on the base?
d How many faces, vertices and edges has an octagonal pyramid?

10. The cone is a special pyramid.
   How many faces, vertices and edges does it have?

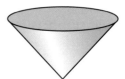

Drawing 3-D shapes

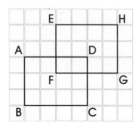 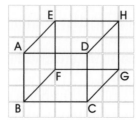 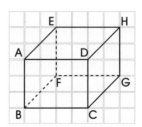

Draw two identical rectangles one up and to the right of the other.

Join the *matching* vertices of the rectangles.

Decide which edges are hidden and make them dotted lines.

B

1. In the cuboid above, AB = 3 cm, AD = 4 cm and AE = 2 cm.

   a State the length and breadth of face:
      i FEHG   ii DHGC   iii BFGC.
   b Name four edges 3 cm long.
   c A spider runs along the edges from B to H by the shortest route. How far did it run?

2. a Copy each diagram onto squared paper.
   b Add just enough lines to make it look like a prism.
   c Say what kind of prism it is.

i	ii	iii	iv
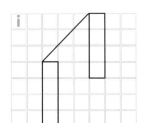	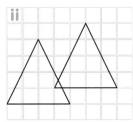	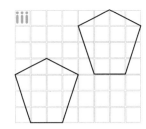	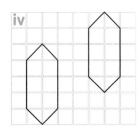

3. You can also draw pictures of pyramids.

   a Follow these steps on squared paper.

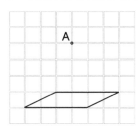

Draw a base and apex.

Join vertices of base to apex.

Make hidden edges dotted lines.

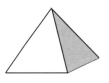

Or rub them out and shade.

   b Copy and complete the pictures of these pyramids. Say what type of pyramid each is.

i	ii	iii
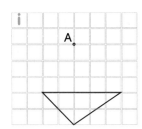	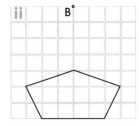	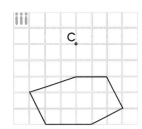

3 ▸ Nets

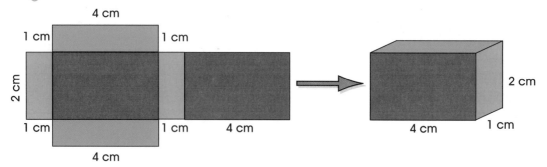

4 cm
1 cm   1 cm
2 cm
1 cm   1 cm   4 cm
4 cm

2 cm
4 cm   1 cm

When this shape is cut out and folded, a cuboid is formed.
The shape is called the **Net** of the cuboid.

  A

1. **a** ❖ Copy the above net onto squared paper.
        ❖ Make the cuboid.
    b How many rectangles of size 2 cm by 4 cm are there in the net?
    c How many rectangles of size 1 cm by 4 cm are there in the net?
    d How many rectangles of size 2 cm by 1 cm are there in the net?
    e What are the dimensions of the final cuboid?

2. If I want to make a cuboid of size 3 cm by 4 cm by 5 cm I will make a net
    that has 2 rectangular faces of 3 cm by 4 cm, two of 3 cm by 5 cm and
    two of 4 cm by 5 cm.

    a On squared paper draw the net described.
    b make the cuboid with the net.

3. Make the net of a cuboid that is:

    a 8 cm by 4 cm by 3 cm
    b 5 cm by 2 cm by 4 cm
    c 1 cm by 5 cm by 6 cm.

4. Three of the following diagrams are nets of cubes.

    a   **b**   **c**   **d**

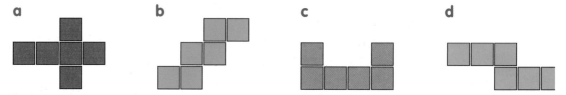

    Use squared paper to help you copy the diagrams.
    Cut them out to discover the one that is not the net of a cube.

5. This is the net of a little cubical box in which sweets are sold. Each edge is 3 cm long.
The grey shapes are tabs, added for the purposes of gluing the box together.

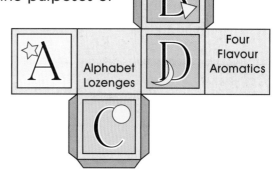

   a Draw the net onto squared paper.
   b Form the box.
   c What is the volume of the finished box?

◆ Investigate

There are actually eleven different nets of the cube. Four are used in questions 4 and 5.
Can you find the other seven? Draw them on squared paper.

4 ▸ Skeleton Models

Solids can be easier to study if you have a model … and even easier if you can see through the model.

If you see a new factory or store being built you can see how cubes and cuboids are used in buildings.

In maths, models made from straws do the job. They are called skeleton models.

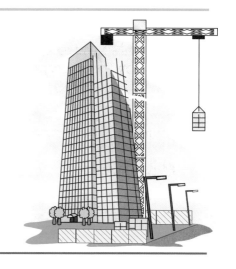

1. Here is a skeleton model of a cuboid.

   a How many straws are needed of length:
      i 12 cm   ii 4 cm   iii 8 cm?
   b If the straws are held together by pieces of tape, how many pieces are needed?
   c Using straws (perhaps made using rolled up paper), construct the model.

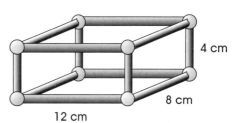

4 cm

8 cm

12 cm

2. The teacher wants a model of a litre. He wants a cube of side 10 cm.

    a How many pieces of straw are needed?
    b How many corner connectors?
    c Make of model of the litre.

Challenge

Using newspapers for making 'straws' make a cubic metre.
When it is built, just imagine you are looking at a million cubic
centimetres!

3. **a** Construct the following skeleton models of these cuboids:

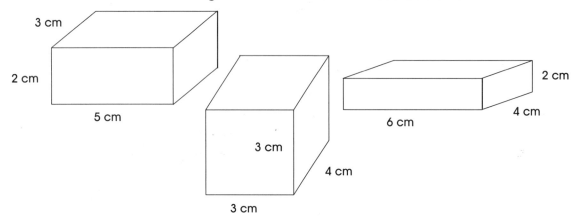

    b Give the volume of each.

4. Using skeleton models you can 'see' features
    that are otherwise hidden.
    In this model, the red line BG runs through
    the heart of the cuboid – it is called a
    space diagonal.

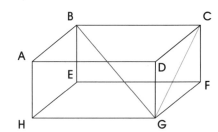

    a There are four space diagonals in a
       cuboid. Name the missing three.
    b How many faces has a cuboid? So how many face diagonals are
       there?
    c Name the face diagonals on the bottom of the cuboid.

Have you found out how many faces Big Ben has?

Think again! Big Ben is the bell in the clock tower!